THE MODERATOR

Valley of Human Struggle

BRAXTON KING

WESTBOW
PRESS®
A DIVISION OF THOMAS NELSON
& ZONDERVAN

THE HOLY BIBLE, NEW INTERNATIONAL VERSION®, NIV® Copyright © 1973, 1978, 1984, 2011 by Biblica, Inc.® Used by permission. All rights reserved worldwide.

Scriptures marked KJV are taken from the KING JAMES VERSION (KJV): KING JAMES VERSION, public domain.

WestBow Press books may be ordered through booksellers or by contacting:

WestBow Press
A Division of Thomas Nelson & Zondervan
1663 Liberty Drive
Bloomington, IN 47403
www.westbowpress.com
1 (866) 928-1240

Because of the dynamic nature of the Internet, any web addresses or links contained in this book may have changed since publication and may no longer be valid. The views expressed in this work are solely those of the author and do not necessarily reflect the views of the publisher, and the publisher hereby disclaims any responsibility for them.

Any people depicted in stock imagery provided by Thinkstock are models, and such images are being used for illustrative purposes only. Certain stock imagery © Thinkstock.

ISBN: 978-1-5127-7128-2 (sc)
ISBN: 978-1-5127-7127-5 (e)

Library of Congress Control Number: 2017900233

Print information available on the last page.

WestBow Press rev. date: 03/02/2017

CONTENTS

FOREWORD

The author has written this book and has given it a title that intrigues me. But it is the sub-title that drove me back toward the idea of slavery It took me out of the city and carried me into the valley of struggling people. He first states his purpose of existence, and then he states his reason for bringing our imagination to the point of freedom and success. I don't know if I enjoy reading this book or not. But I learned from the pages as to what God expect. I must be honest with myself; these pages contain the purpose of God in reaching out into the communities that are struggling with reality. Reaching and finding people who wants to live a life beyond their daily struggle, where prayer mean little to them. Fear, doubt, and un-repented sin, keep those in the valley from worshipping near the cross. The author makes a bold move that if it backfires, the moderator does not have a chance. The reversal marriage is a dangerous move to make, primarily, because many will misunderstand its concept. When I think about the whole process I tremble. The deliverance team is biblical, but for us is it practical? Do we want to be Christians enough to be obedient to God's word? Sometime I think the author is a little touched in the head. And yet, you cannot find anything wrong with his approach to transforming the association from a lame duck organization, to a spiritual organization who stands near God, eager to be obedient to God's word.

I like the book, I would not want to be the deacon who must come up under this brother's insight. His visit to the second and third heaven, and the hearing of God's voice in his son's native language of Arabic. There are his good intentions to call on this old bitten pastor, who lives at the edge of turning around for God, and transformed him into his lead man. The way that his people were chosen, over and beyond their expectation; beyond their imagination he reach into their mind and heart, and pulled out men and women for God's purpose. He never left the protection of God's direction even when he is short of his dedication. I bow my head and tip my cap to this author for what he is trying to do. I give him all the respect in the world. The animals and how they were placed in the book kept me looking ahead for for intrigue. Then again why not, it appears that is found in the book. I find some doubt in places where doubt should not be. That is not the authors fault, for doubt may come from my inner beliefs, and the teaching that I have been taught over the years. I hope that I will never be asked to be The Moderator. The struggle grinds me to the bottom of the dirt pit, in the valley of human struggle.

Rev. F.E.Randall'

BIBLIOGRAPHY

Blue, Ronald W. (Master Your Money) Nashville, Tennessee. Thomas Nelson Publishers)1997.

Harre, Alan F. (Closing The Back Door) ST. Louis, Mo.63118. Concordia Publishing. 1984.

Maxwell, John C. (The Success Journal) Nashville, Tenn. Thomas Nelson Publishers.1997

Segler, Franklin M. (Christian Worship Its Theology and Practice:) Nashville, Tenn. Broasman Press. 1967.

Naxwell, John C.(Laws of Leadership -The 21 Irrefutable) Nashville, Tenn. Thomas Nelson Pub.2007.

McIntosh, Gary. Martin, Glen. (Keeping Them and finding Them) Nashville, Tenn. Broadman-Holman 1992.

Weeks, Dudley. Phd. (Conflict Resolution) New York, NEew York. Jeremy P. Tarcher.

Coleman, Robert E. (The Master Plan of Evengelism) Old Tappan New Jersey, Flemming H. Revelle1963.

Braxton King (Call of The Locust) Succorer Pub. 2321 W. Pioneer Pky. #325.Grand Prairie, Texas 7051

Paul R. Jackson (The Doctrine and administration of The Church.) Regular Baptist Press 1300 North Meacham Rd.

Braxton King (The Brother Up Next.) West Bow Press 1613 Liberty Drive Bloomington, In.47403 2011

Harmon, Frank and Ida (Pigs in The Parlor.) Kirkwood, Mo. Impact Books Inc.1973

Deacon Albert L. Black. President of the brotherhood auxiliary, Missionary General Baptist Convention of Texas, Austin, Texas

Deacon Edward King Chairman of the deacon board of Mt. olive Baptist church, Sudan.Texas. Former Director of Brotherhood Union Cap/Rock District Association.

INTRODUCTION

The Cap/Rock District Association, at one time was considered the crown jewel of the State of Texas. A few money hungry preachers and messengers came together and drove it into the ground. Then one day its moderator made a decision that shattered the concept of the fellowship of local churches. When the men walked away, the buildings fell down, then it rested in piles of lumber upon a dirty ground. The men were the heart of the association, but they were supported by the love of their wives.

They walked away, some with their heads down in sorrow, some carried bitterness and hate that they could not find forgiveness for. Others tried and failed to rebuild the once monument among Black Baptist Churches. There were no funeral or formal service to agree to its demise, but now the property that once housed the association, lay bare with nothing on it. A bitter person, who carries their bitterness in the secret of their hearts, seldom spoke of the good times that they once had. Those who caused the demise and lost of respect have long been in their graves, their tenure has come to an end. Memories of great times and services that rocked that part of the country could still be remembered. Even now it brought tears to some of the old women, who respected their men and supported them to the last Amen.

Dr. Therious Edward King and his wife Eartha lives comfortably in this moderate built four bed room home with a office large enough for a cooperate vice president. He had everything that a southern

Baptist preacher wanted except success. He has a beautiful wife with three children. The wife is an educator who is well respected in her profession. The both of them enjoy playing in their garden at the rear of the house. They make it a point to keep something green growing within the wall's of the fence. The house sets on three acres of land, outside the garden is a couple of well manicured rolling acres.

(1)

Rev. King did not have a drinking problem, but when he had more problems than he could handle, he would go into his office and lock the door. The wife knew what was going on, she would never bother him. They did not have the kind of marriage that was expected of a pastor and his wife. But they were respected in the community where they lived. They always put up a good front, but they did not try to fool anyone, and they always made it a habit to respect each other. They were a model couple outside the fences, but it was inside the fences that was driving Sis.King toward a nervous condition. The love and affection was missing, and she was missing a part of her life that she had started with. O, yes, they were the model couple, that was going somewhere.

The kids came soon after they were married. It was then that the church did not pay enough for them to live on. He had started to work for a large sale company that paid him well. He enjoyed his family, well most of the time. He was excited about his job, the church was doing well. He was not a courting man, but he liked the way that women looked at him. It was being successful was the central thought on his mind. The company where he worked liked his leadership skills, they liked his personal skills, but for a preacher he seems to have desired more of the world than what was in the church. But his leadership skills kept the church growing, there were exciting things happening with this membership.

The deacons were all over sixty years old, they were accustomed to real worship and reverence. They liked the hymns, and something that meant something to the soul. They believed that devotion was necessary for the beginning of a worship service. The old chairman, when you mentioned worship said the same thing over, and over, and over again. He would say: When I think about worship, I think about Jesus, "When they saw him, they worshiped him". He WOULD SAY to worship is to bow down in awe; to pay divine honors to God in humble, reverent homage. Then he would say; there are three essentials in worship. Faith, the people believed ... ... then they bowed their heads and worshiped." The spirit, he said, as if he wanted every person in the world to hear him. "They worshiped him in spirit --spiritual worship is worship directed by the indwelling Holy Spirit" And then he would say last but not lest, "They that worship must worship him in spirit and truth." Jesus Christ is truth.

Therefore there can be no pretense or hypocrisy in true worship. He would hit his right hand on his right knee, "Without devotion, there is no true worship.

CHAPTER #1

The Struggle to Comprehend

("And for me, that utterance may be given unto me,
that I may open my mouth boldly, to make known
the mystery of the gospel." (Eph. 6:19)

Time had eroded Rev. King's popularity and on today, three days
before thanksgiving he was battling the possibility that he may lose
the church. This evening he was battling with the possibility of
losing his church and his wife. (Even though the church was doing
well, there was a lot of un-satisfaction among the membership. He
believed that if he was at the church on Sunday and Wednesday,
what he done with the rest of his time, was his business. He was
good with the young and young adults. He knew how to share with
them what they wanted to hear. But these members are young and
they needed their money to pay bills. The mortgage take a vacation
every once in a while. The people who gave the most money were
those who did not like his style. The fact of the matter, his job took
more of his time than a pastor should have to give.

His job, his high living, and the conflict at the church were
hurting his family life. He and his wife were growing further and
further apart. She told herself that she did not care whatever he done
was all-right with her. But there were times that she wanted to lay
comfortable in his arms. She wanted to feel his touch, listen to his

sweet words of encouragement. Even though she knew that he would be lying, she wanted to hear him to say that he loved her, give her a tender kiss and a big smile. She just wanted to know that he was her man, her friend and her lover. It was not a talked about thing between them, but it had come up in the silence of the bedroom. His wife had already told him if he lost the church, she was gone.

Things with them was kind of raggedy, it was nothing serious, just a few little things that got on each others nerves. Rev. King wanted to be a big man in the state convention, national convention and the district association. He liked for people to look up to him and call him, Dr. King. His spiritual life was not where it should be, not for a preacher. He was aware of it, but he thought that he had enough of Jesus Christ to get into the kingdom. Yes, he was aware that he was not the strongest pastor in this part of the country. He was aware that he had a couple of weak spots, which was kept secret from most people that he knew. His wife loved him, or she thought that she did. But she had grown tired of him desiring to accomplish great things. There were times she would slip into his medicine cabinet, closed the bedroom door and put a buzz on. She did not do this often, and then she would get on her knees and cry out to God for forgiveness.

Dr. Therious Edward King, had a beautiful wife, three kids he adored, and a garden that always had some thing green growing, on the two acre site where they lived. He knew that they were living above their means, but he had to show people that he had arrived. It was the battle inside of him that gave him trouble. A battle that God stood on the outside looking in unto him. King had some excellent traits for leadership, he was smart, and friendly, but he was not humble.

His desire to conquer the world before he left here, rode a hard bargain in his conscious mind. A battle that was fought daily, but there were seldom winners. King did not have a drinking problem, but when things got bad, he would go into his office and calm his nerves. He did not want to think about the world problems. Neither tries to solve the problem of paying for what he did have. He would go into the room and set in his office and pass out before he went to asleep. His wife would lock the door, to make sure that no one saw him, especially the family and church members.

There was nothing about Rev. King that would cause another human being to stop and observe. On the other hand some women found him desirable. One could not see his determination, desire and his strength not yet captured. You had to know the man. From the inside out he was one of the most determined men who walked these shores of earthly success. His thoughts of success drove him on a daily bases. Some time one could see him doubled over as if he had a terrible stomach pain. Tears would run down his cheek as if he lost one of his children. His family at times could not stop him; he was like a mad dog. But when he left home he was always composed and in control.

Rev. King is a minor part of the Cap/Rock District Association of Texas. And less than a minor part of the City Wide Brotherhood in the city of Dallas. The man knew his lesson, and knew it well. He knew his limitations in delivery of the gospel. But overall he was kind of a loner looking to be successful.

It was about two days before thanksgiving that he walked into his office leaving the door wide open. He sat down in his large black comfortable leather chair.

This trip to the office was different; he was not trying to forget Anything; he was wondering how he was going to get out of this mess. His church was on the line. The church was not in conflict about the Bible or spiritual things. Little things that seem not to make a different had grown into mountain. The membership took their silly arguments home, and they took sides, it did not matter right or wrong, they all stayed together in their wrongness. Yes it did affect the whole church. His wife was thinking about leaving.

He was not sure if she was leaving him or the church. About that time she walked to the door of the office; she wanted to know if he wanted the door closed. He said no. She stood there for a moment, and then she asked him if anything was wrong. For a while he did not say a word, finally he turned to face her. "Eartha this may be the only time that you will have the freedom to walk away and I will not say a word " he looked down toward the floor, "I don't know what I would do without you, but I love you too much to put you through all of this ambitious folly. If you chose to leave I will not leave this room until you have packed and left the house. She looked at him.

"We have come too far to turn back now, we have been through too many things, too many storms, walked down too many rocky roads, approached too many rivers that if we were not together, we would never have crossed them. The nights that you were sleeping, I was on my knees begging God to help us. The nights that you stayed out until just before day; the times that you would not let me question you as to where you were.

I turned my face toward the wall and cried many hot flowing tears; recalling the voices of young women in the church talking about your love making. O I found out later that they were lying, but at first I did not know. Where were we going, what was in front of us, what could we expect. Without knowing where we are going and where we were going to stay. If you can see your way to let God control your life, you would make a good husband, productive father and a fine pastor. Everything that you need, is here, I thought once about leaving, but if I left you, where would you go. Between your home, your church, your wife and kids everything that you want to accomplish is within your reach." She went over, put her arms around him. "I'm not going anywhere"

Eartha walked to the door that she had walked through, looking back at him, she said. "I thought more than once about leaving, but then where would I go. What would I tell God, how could I repent and be forgiven. No, I'm going to stay and pray to God one day you will hear his call.

One day you will respect him for who he is. That you will remember what he has done for you. Maybe some where you can remember the sermons that you preach, 'Faith in Jesus Christ and

4

believing in the word of God. She turned and closed the door gently behind her. The phone rang as she closed the door. He seldom answered the phone, so she answered the phone with the kindness of angels. They talked for a moment, and then she put it on hold. His wife walked back into the office, picked up the phone and handed it to him.

He looked at her as she walked out the room. After closing the door, her little son was running through the room, he stopped and waved at her, "Hi, mommie" She smiled and waved back at him. It was then that she noticed how much her son resembles his father. Even if she left him, he would always be there in his son. So she will stay to see what the end will be like. He was surprise, that the caller was the president of the state convention.

He shared with Rev. King that the moderator of the Cap/Rock district association had suffered a heart attack this afternoon. The hospital staff was not expecting him to live. He also passed on that the moderator had decided to give up his position with the district and he wanted him to take over. He informed him that they were aware that he was not the next person in line for the position, but the next two people were not structured enough to carry on in this short period of time.

We will give you three years to get this association back on its feet. You will have to choose your own staff. There was a long pause, "King, with all that you will have coming in financially, and you have finally arrived, as moderator. We will see to it that you will make enough to pay your bills, and enjoy the kind of lifestyle that you desire. We will expect you to bring us your plan before me and my staff before the 30th of October of next year. He was surprised and pleasantly shocked to learn that he had been made Moderator of the district association of Texas. He had been informed that he would be able to choose his staff, but to be careful in his expenses, because what he takes home will be balanced with the money at his disposal in the association. Rev. King accepted the offer and thanked him for sharing this information.

He was so excited that he could hardly breathe. He could not believe it; finally he had what he wanted. He thought the church would not dare let him go while he is the moderator of the district. He got up slowly, pinching himself physiologically. He had arrived, the time was now, and he must make the best of this chance.

He walked over to the large glass window, looking out he could see sleet and rain mixed together and falling to the ground. Occasionally a piece of the ice would jump up and roll over to another place. The road that ran by his house to the right was a small white church with a staple on top of it. It was small, but in the past two years they had lost almost half of their congregation. They were barely keeping their doors open. To his left on the side of the hill was a larger church, and they had lost about a third of its membership.

He thought to himself; what is the reason for the falling away of the churches membership. He knew there were many reasons, but if he was to choose three or four reasons for the demise; it would be the failure of many mainstream Christian churches to embrace social movements of recent decades--from Gay rights to women's equality to peace activism, including women preachers. These and more has alienated young people who see the contradiction with Jesus teaching of tolerance. The statistic continue to pour into the knowledge of man.

The churches in America that was once thriving and considered mainline are shrinking and struggling to stay alive. He thought for a moment; people leave church because they need less drama in their lives. Some leave church because of unresolved conflict, some leave because they get turned off by social climbing, cliques, and nepotism, some leave church because they're looking for something authentic, some leave church because they don't find Jesus, others leave when there are not qualified teachers to teach And leaders in place for the growth of the church. Why now, at a time that he is suppose to be happy, exciting about what lie ahead of him, the dark side keep coming up. It did not matter how hard he tried to keep it away, it just would not stay.

He had been off the phone a little while struggling with his conscious, as if it was his fault. This had nothing to do with him, he kept telling himself, and this is much larger than I am. God and Satan are the only real powers in this world, why can't they handle this conflict. It is out of reach of man, we are powerless to set this straight. He thought about the passage in the book of Revelation, 12:10-12, ISB "Now salvation, and strength and the kingdom of our God and the power of his Christ have come, for the accuser of your brethren, who accused them before our God day and night, has been cast down. And they overcame him by the blood of the lamb and by the word of their testimony, and they did not love their lives to the death.

Therefore rejoice O Heavens, and you who dwell in them! Woe to the inhabitants of the earth and the sea!

For the devil has come down to you having great wrath, because he knows that he has a short time." King thought to himself, if he is too much for those in heaven, where the residents are spiritual, what we can do with him here on earth, where the residents are physical.

Rev. King was still looking at the wintry fall weather, when the phone rang. It startled him at first, for he was not sure where the phone was. Finally he picked the phone up; it was a friend of his that lived in Houston, Texas. He had heard that the position of moderator had been offered to him. He wanted to tell him not to take the position that he was being set up, He wanted to let him know that some of his so called friends was on the other team to take over when he failed. That they did not expect him to last more than a year or two at the most.

He told Therious that it was a set up; they needed a fall guy to set a foundation underneath the association. When that was completed, they were going to move him and put in their own people. His friend informed him that a group of people had already been chosen for the job. He also told King that he had only a selected group of people to choose from. All the talented people who knew something about associations and conventions had been contacted and informed not

7

to allow King to talk them into helping him. This was the kind of association which held I-o-u. And they were not afraid to call them in. He was allowed to choose his staff and workers, and even he did not have any idea as to who they would be.

His selection into the position of Moderator of the Cap/Rock District Association Was designed for him to fail. They respected his ability to lead, but they did not like him as a leader. Making him moderator was to throw him to the wolves, make the association fails, where they could pick it up from the ashes, and drive it to success. But there were a strange thing about all of this. The association was presently on its back at this time, no one had any respect for its ability to function. They had drained all the money from the treasurer. People had stopped coming to the main event in the first or second week in August. The few people who came had positions and now that the money had run out, they would not be coming back. There were people around him that bragged on him patted him on the back and called him Doctor. They laughed inside because he was a sure failure.

Therious knew that they expected him to fail, and he was equally determined to succeed.

At this moment failure was not his major problem, he had more than one health concern, he had kind of threw a few words her way about his health, but he had not told her about his prostrate cancer and the concern his doctors had about his colane. He had not had either one checked by a specialist. He knew that there were a possibility that if let go unchecked he could lose his life. He had a hard time convincing himself that he was going to die from cancer. With this situation that lie ahead of him, he had to be concerned about his health. He knew that he must tell his wife of his condition. The church must also know, but there were no reason for him to tell the state convention. But his wife, he had to tell her, they had to discuss his condition and figure out what they were going to do. What he would have to do at home was almost as important as being in the hospital.

The question to him was how was he to do it. There were too many pastors who were on the other side, people with influence, many of them not saved, some did not even care. There were some who did not believe in heaven or hell. They believed that when one dies his life is over with, to them there is no here after. Many among the leadership had learned to accept same sex marriage. It seem as if the same sex marriages always had money. They believed that each person had their own call concerning the entrance to heaven. It was from this group that they wanted to expose the people with this kind of leadership.

King sat in his comfortable recliner, watching an old western movie. "THE LAST TRAIN FROM GUN HILL." It was just before midnight and every thing out side had taken its place for the night. But as for him nearing sleep had not bothered to calm him down. He wanted this to be a man's association, where men drew men. He wanted this association to be the crown jewel of the associations. Where men from other associations would look upon the men from the Cap-Rock. Men of this association could feel proud in their knowledge of their calling. They did not have to guess, they knew their bible and what God had intended for them to do with that knowledge. Men who found that their relationship with their wives or sufficiently other loved them and looked upon them with pride.

Senior women who was not afraid to discuss biblical things with younger men and women. With people of other denomination without fear of not knowing what they would be talking about. He had an idea of what he wanted to happen, he wanted his administration to be the foundation of a great body of believers.

When the movie went off, he did not replace it with another movie; he replaced it with simple music, music from the fifties and sixties. He did not want to hear anyone talking or singing. He just wanted to hear soft music, at this point, music of the past. On his way back to his seat, he stopped long enough to observe the three books that was always on his desk. This time they had a special place somewhere in his future. He let his hand rest on them, and then went onto his seat with a smile on his face.

Finally he reached over and picked the books up and spread them out in front of him. he looked on his desk and picked up a book entitled, "THE BROTHER UP NEXT". He had always admired the book because a friend of his had written the \novel. He thumbed through the book with interest, his mind picking up on some of the topics; Financial responsibility-Respect of God-Obedient/commitment-Reliable evangelism, and it rested upon the final chapter "Conflict Resolution". He then picked up the all mighty Bible; this is the book of books-and knowledge of knowledge. Finally he picked up "The Administration and Doctrine of The Church, by Paul R. Jackson. If he could get every person involved with the association to study these three books he would be able to teach from them, he would be proud.

Here he said out loud, here is the answer to what I want to do. But I must choose men and a few women to fulfill the key responsibility of this movement. I need one to be like Dr. Smith and Rev. Douglas of Shiloh Baptist Church in the bottom. But he knew that both of these men has passed on into eternity. He needed men who was built and grown on the foundation of those two men. He needed seven people who walks with God, where the Holy Spirit, God the father and his son call's them friends.

He needed a plan that was brought to him in a vision from God and a church goal that heaven find favorable for success. There were a book lying on his desk, the back part of the desk. He could not see the title, but he could not keep his eyes away from the book cover. He could not reach for it, but it occupied his every thought.

He thought to himself, what could be in that book that can shadow the vision of God, Develop a plan that God loves, and set afire a goal the membership would work hard to accomplish. He would have to develop more believers to discipleship, and sinners to the way of the cross.

CHAPTER #2

The Development Foundation

(Study to show thyself approved unto God, a
workman that needeth not to be ashamed, rightly
dividing the word of truth.) (11 Tim.2:15)

The foundation at Dr. Therious Edward King church and the doctrine
of Jesus Christ would rest and abide on his shoulders. But what does
this book have to do with the development of a great association.
As he thumbed through the book a familiar scripture broke into his
weary mind. Matthew 28:19-20.NIV. "Go ye therefore, and teach
all nations, baptizing them in the name of the father, and of the
son, and of the Holy Ghost: Teaching them to observe all things
whatsoever I have commanded you: and lo, I am with you always
even unto the end of the world. Amen." But it was the matching
scripture, about the same event that choked his vivid mind. Mark
16:15-18.NIV "He said unto them, "Go ye into all the world, and
preach the gospel to every creature.

He that believeth and is baptized shall be saved; but he that
believeth not shall be damned. And these signs shall follow them
who believe; in my name shall they cast out devils; they shall speak
with new tongues.

They shall take up serpents; and if they drink any deadly thing,
it shall not hurt them; they shall lay hands on the sick, and they

shall recover" …" He looked at the book that he now recognize as the Holy Bible and thought to him self. My people are afraid of the command that God has given between these pages.

Rev, King looked at the two scripture and wandered were there something behind those words that he could not see. He had accepted the new terminology, witness as you go. There is no doubt that we should be a witness wherever we go. But this phase builds within the membership a laziness that will give them an out, where all they have to do is ask people to come to church, or ask them if they are Christians, maybe they will tell them that they need Jesus Christ as their Savior and Lord. He couldn't get the words out of his mind, "Tell them to obey all that I have commanded thee." The words began to come to him. The words that did not come from the bible, and yet they came rushing into his mind. He was not sure if he had heard them before, but they were pounding the back of his mind like crazy. He knew that it was God. A fire had been lit in his stomach, and the mind could not hold the intentions of the soul. It was there, but then was it there, the words might have been there but the understanding had not found true meaning in his humble spirit. He felt as if he had it all, but it had not come together. But knowing God as he knew him, when the time came it would be there.

There seem to have been an explosion in the mind that caused him to leap to his feet. But once there he was not sure where he was. What three areas' will the association accept and stand on. There have to be a protection level, to keep the people away from fear. A level where Jesus Christ rules with a hand of love, grace, and mercy. And then there will be alternates protection that guide the people to its accomplishment. Evangelism-sharing the gospel to the loss; giving them an opportunity to accept him or reject the commands of God. Stewardship-using God given resources to accomplish God given responsibility. Spiritual Gifts- To answer the question, what is it that God wants you to do. He looked through the book, The Brother Up Next. There in the table of contents lie part of the answer. It was enough for the message, but he would have to find a carrier. (Men and women to carry the message with a personality, the attitude of knowledge and the motive of wisdom that drives the message home.)

His mind went back to Matthew 28:19-20. What would he teach his followers about a passage that is so familiar, one that most all leaders know by heart? What can he say that would drive home the meaning and responsibility of each believer. (There have to be a thought provoking catch word or phrase that would stand them on their feet). He knew then that he would have the message ready, a powerful message that drives a spike through the heart of men. Words and meanings that cause a man to set and think and to have an earthly fear of God.

With his mind on the scripture, he thought about Christ having finished his calling on this earth. He is now getting ready to depart a mean and cruel earth for a kingdom in heaven with his father. He took time out while they could see him; he then gave them two things which is the same and yet not a like. He knew that if the world was to have heard the word of God, it would start with them and then spread to the utmost part of the world. Believers would have to carry the word with a compassion for the saving of souls. No one else can carry the word of God except those who have been born again, have the love of God within their souls, and with this true repentance that cause them to be friends of God.

The words in Matthew 28:19-20 and Mark 16:15-18? They are not only words of encouragement and some directions for man to follow. He left with them a command for believers to obey and teach others to obey. To disobey a command of God is sin.

The disobedience of this command requires that when the believer disobeys it, he has to repent of the sin that he has disobeyed. True repent-stop not doing it to sharing the gospel. These words are also a covenant agreement with God, his son and the Holy spirit-to the believer. This covenant has been signed in the blood of Jesus-giving the believer all the protection that he needs. When the believer breaks the covenant it become a un=repented sin. It is a sin that one is aware of, and when he prays before the Lord, to forgive him of all his sins known and unknown, this un-repented sin is not covered. This un-repented sin has to be repented of, for it stand alone. Why? It is first a command from God to his people. Second it is a covenant agreement written in blood, the breaking of it requires repentance. One have to confess the sin of not sharing the word of God, and make the decision to share the gospel as long as he can.

Let us look a little closer to the word repentance in its truest sense: Repentance must involve both change of mind and change of action. When we sin we may well do something to ourselves and to others which cannot be undone. Forgiveness does not abolish the consequence of what we have done but it puts us right with God. When repentance come something happens for the past. There is God's forgiveness for what lies behind. Let us be quite clear that the consequence of sins are not wiped out because we ask God to forgive us. Not even God can do that. When repentance comes something happens for the future. We receive the gift of the Holy Spirit and in that power we can win battles we never thought to win or resist things which by ourselves we would have been powerless to resist. Repentance is bound to hurt, for it involves the bitter realization that the way we were following is wrong. It is bound to disturb, because it means a complete reversal of life.

Rev. King will have a problem with repentance and the born-again experience. But that is a battle that he must fight with himself. Let us look briefly at this born-again experience. When a man become a Christian, there comes into his life a change so radical and so decisive that he can only be said to be born again. It happens to a man, not by his own efforts, but when he yields himself to be possessed and occupied and recreated by the Spirit within him. It is the creative word of God in Jesus Christ and in God's book which brings about this rebirth in a man's life. This disobedience to God's command should not be with a born-again believer. But as long as we are human we will fail, get up, and fail again. Only God can keep us from falling.

Many sanctuary dwellers raises their voice in worship loaded down with the un-repented sin of not being obedient to the word of God. At some point the load gets so heavy that one's salvation is hid behind the callus wall of un-repented intentional disobedience. The command of God should not be taken lightly, it could build from neglect to God does he know what he is doing. That our lives rest under our intentions and not the love of God. Over time our disobedience bring on an anger that develops in the wrath of God upon our lives. Because of where we are, who we are, and who's we say that we are, will eventually bring on the anger and wrath of God upon our lives.

Why have the church in the presence of God made such an effort not to share the word of God so that those who does not know him will not have a chance to accept him or reject him.

Only believers can share the gospel of Jesus Christ with the lost. No one else has the testimony and have experienced the power of God in their souls. Church members who attend church weekly, deacons who pray and sing-taking care of the administration of the church, Preachers and pastor with hand rose from the pulpit. The teachers of the word-Sunday school, brotherhood, mission etc. Move about on Sunday morning and on Wednesday night with no intention of sharing the good news. Many are not aware that each time a chance come for them to share the good news and they don't do it. It becomes an extra weight to carry until they fail again, and then another weight is added to journey.

Why have the church failed to carry out Gods instructions. He has made it clear what he wants us to do. If we do nothing else, he wants us to share the good news. Many teachers and pastors have deliberately refused to teach the obeying of Gods word. They do not find it important to snatch lost souls from the world. And while they are doing this they themselves are moving closer to giving up their once salvation, that great love, that commanding spirit which drives us to be obedient, into the murky waters of Hell. When the practice of disobedience become a part of one's total life. The spirit that moves him may not be from God. If we follow Satan and his angels when we know we are wrong, we give Satan more power in our lives than we give God. Satan will fool us into believing that all is well with God. He will give us things to continue our disobedience with God. God has allowed our spiritual ear to be obedient to our desires. That cause us to move into a space in time of un=-belief.

What is it about the church that seem to feel as if God does not know what he is doing? That it was ok back then, but today is different. How can we so easily be disobedient to God's word in sharing the only printed truth that heaven has to offer us? How can we say no before we get down to pray; but after our father, we are true to his word. We have got to be kidding ourselves. We cannot serve two Gods at the same time, we cannot be faithful to both. When trouble pounds us into submission the true and living God is the one we cry out to, begging for his help. But when we don't' want to do something we find an excuse to bed it down.

What is the church thinking when they are confronted with the possibility that they are in a sin nature, when they fail to share the good news.

I believe they have lost their way-they have forgotten who Jesus the Christ is. They have forgotten their commitment to an all mighty God. They have forgotten what the son of God went through to give us a chance to enter the kingdom. They forget that yesterday's mothers and fathers, grand fathers and grand mothers so depended upon God almighty that when food was short they did not worry, when the children did not have clothes, mother and grand mother would be hanging their clothes out on a close line humming and crying-believing that God would bring them through. Prayers rang out from their inner self pleading with God for the help that they knew would come. What is happening to us?

We have forgotten who God is, what he has done for us. We have not forgotten his blessings and promises, but we have forgotten the condition for bringing them into our lives. Let us for a few moments see if we can draw the mind down to Christian reality. And re-discover the love, faith, born again experience, and maybe we can find repentance and forgiveness that have been escaping a life that have fallen away from the main road. In the book of Matthew 7:21-23,niv "Not everyone who says to me, Lord, Lord, will enter into the kingdom of Heaven. But only he who does the will of my father. Many will say to me on that day, Lord, Lord, did we not prophesy in your name and in your name drive out demons and perform many miracles?" Then I will tell them plainly, I never knew you. Away from me, you evildoers." "Enter through the narrow gate. For wide is the gate and broad is the road that leads to destruction, and many enters through it. But small is the gate and narrow the road that leads to life and only a few find it. Matt.7:13-14."

There need not be a reason for a Christian to lie down with the weight of un-repented sin in their lives. Especially, the sin of disobedience to (a merciful and loving God) of an all mighty God. Who gave this one command on his way back to his father signed in his own blood? and under the command of a God who gave his life that all of his creations may one day live with him in heaven. It tears his heart to pieces to observe those who has their qualifications in His word who once said, Yes, Lord. But now in the closing of time near the tribulation period, they have forgotten him. It did not happen overnight, it happen slowly and it seem so innocent. But this disobedient to the son of God as he is watching over us. As he is sustaining us while we cannot take care of ourselves. What little sleep that does show up and we are unaware of living, he sustains us over our disobedient self.

When Jesus and his disciples were in the area of Caesarea Philippi. They stopped beneath a tree to rest their weary body. He could see that there were some unbelief and doubt in their weary souls of his disciples. There were something that they did not understand, but they did not share it with the master. While they were resting their tied legs and back, he asked them, who do people say that I the son of man am? They said Jeremiah, Elijah, John the Baptist or one of the prophets. Then he asked them, what about you, who do you, say that I the son of man am. I believe it was peter saying, 'Thy art the Christ, the son of the living God'. He looked at them as they were observing him, then he said, "Flesh and blood did reveal this unto you but my father which is in heaven. not cause you to recognize me, but it was my father in heaven'.

All spiritual answers to spiritual questions and conflicts must come from heaven. That is the place where God the Father, His son Jesus Christ and the Holy Spirit resides. If there is an inkling of doubt about your salvation or your relationship with the good Lord; if there are scriptures that share the truth's of the gospel and if you are having a difficult time understanding what God is saying to you, and if you desire to be faithful to him, regardless of the circumstance, He remain available to share with you the truth of his divine presence in your life. If there is un-repented sin that had been in your life for many years, and your-father forgive you for all my sins, are words but not a part of your prayer? Tell him what the sin is, recognize him for who he is, and name the sin before him. Walk away from the sin with his help, turn your back on it, take up your cross daily and follow him.

Rev. King thought about the condition of the of the church and the district association. He thought about the pastor and deacons who allowed such a conflict to come into the worship place of an all mighty God. Have Christian people forgotten who Jesus is; have they forgotten what he went through for their sake. What about his suffering, his doing good, casting out demon's, healing the sick, causing the blind to see, the lame to walk. Have the church forgotten how he stood before Satan, and was tempted in all ways as we are and yet he did not sin.

A few weeks had passed when he and his disciples stopped at the Mt. of Olives. This was the place where he would stop to pray when he was in this part of the country. He took his disciples to a certain place and left them. Then He and Peter, James and John went a little further, he told the three to stay in this particular place and pray. Then he went a stone throw away bowed down toward the mother dust and cried out to his father. "Father, if you are willing, please take this bitter cup of horror from me, yet not my will, but yours be done." 'An angel from heaven appeared to him and strengthen him. And being In agony, he prayed more earnestly, and his sweat was like drops of blood falling to the ground. He did not stop; he kept on praying that the will of God be done.

A few days later the council held court in a dark room at night. It was here that they found him guilty of saying that he is the Son of God. This was to be a crime that required death. The Romans did not want to take the life of Jesus on their word. But God's people said that it required death. When they were told that the Romans would have to release one of the prisoners, they said release Barabbas, but crucify Jesus. They nailed him to an old cross made from an old tree. They took large nails and drove them through his hands.

When day light had come, they put the cross upon his shoulder; and there he walked under the heaviness of the cross of the whole world. When they got to Calvary they raised the cross and stood it into the ground. Jesus was between earth and heaven. The earth had just said crucify him, they did not want him on earth; heaven was not ready for him, for he had not become sin for all of creation. And the father had said that he must go through the suffering before he could come back to be with the father. Around about twelve o'clock darkness spread all over God's creation. There were no light anywhere. Some say that one could ball up his fist and feel the darkness between his fingers.

It is said the darkness that came upon the earth, was because the father could not look upon his son; The son had become sin for all of man kind. He had not sin, he was not disobedient to his father, and he had done no wrong. But if God's creation were to have a chance to eternity with him, his Son had to go through this bitter suffering. It broke his father heart, but this is what sin has done to mankind. Long toward the end of the three hours, he cried out to the father, "Father why has thy forsaken me" He dropped his head into the lock of his shoulders and said "It is finish" He said to the father "Into thy hands I command my spirit." but before he started back to heaven he left a command for his followers to follow. For them not to obey his command would stifle the spread of the gospel and put all that he had done at pearl of disobedient to his father. He took this command, made it into a covenant, then signed the agreement in his own blood. Nothing is as important as sharing the good news for believers, and if they refuse to share, it just maybe they don't know him after all.

He would not leave earth or his disciples without preparing them to share the gospel. All disciples who come after that historic event, takes on the responsibility of sharing the good news. He did not ask us, believers, servants, slaves, friends to share. He said go ye. Then he accepted the invitation of a ride back to his home in heaven. His father who had said well done was waiting on his arrival. God is waiting on us to obey the command of his son, to show the world that we are true followers of the trinity.

One cannot rest easily until he obeys the command that God has given to his followers. A refusal to obey God's will, in time bring on the seven year tribulation period. A time that the church may not be prepared for. Many who attend church on regular bases will not be ready. Matt.7: 13-14.niv "Enter through the narrow gate, for wide is the gate, and broad is the road that leads to destruction, and many enter through it. But small is the gate and narrow the road that lead to life, only a few find it."

In verse 21 of the same chapter, "Not everyone who say to me, Lord, Lord, will enter the kingdom of heaven, but only he who does the will of my father who is in heaven. Many will say to me on that day, Lord, Lord, did we not prophesy in your name and in your name drive out demons and perform many miracles? Then I will tell them plainly, I never knew you. Away from me, you evildoers." People who do not share the gospel of Jesus Christ is in danger of walking down the broad road that lead to destruction.

Rev. King stood up, walk softly over to the window; it is a large plate glass window. His mind is full of questions, and few answers.

Where will he find the people, qualified people? But on the other hand, what are their qualifications. He has to mix men and women unless he is dooming himself to failure. Failure is a word that has no place in his conscious mind, or thoughts on the edge of space in the time we live. Therious finds himself looking out a large plate glass window on the east side of the house. The night lamps are at their best in the early morning. There is just something lovely and lonely about night lights in a city, when they are washing the streets. Through the mist of water and low fog the night lights seem to beg for company that is not coming. So it cast a lighted area down the streets a way's waiting on the man in the brown leather over coat and Dobb hat. When he comes he will be whistling "Rainy night in Georgia". The man may or may not come, no one knows if such a man is stranded somewhere in the city.

He thought to himself, that his mind had run away with him. There were a long hesitation and a dropped head. Where, he thought to himself, where would he get (12) men and women to help him carry this mighty task. When he thought about the twelve people, the twelve disciples came to mind. In the book of Mark 3:13-19 NIV. Jesus went up on a mountainside, and called to him those he wanted, and they came to him. He appointed twelve-designating them apostles -that they might be with him and that he might send them out to preach and to have the authority to drive out demons". Jesus had come to a very important moment in his life and work. He had emerged with his message; he had chosen his method; he had gone through Galilee preaching and healing. By this time he had made a very considerable impact on the public mind.

Now he had to face two practical problems. First he had to find some way of making his message permanent if anything happens to him,, and, and that something would happen he did not doubt. Second he had to find some way of disseminating his message. There were only one way to solve these two problems; he had to choose certain men on whose hearts and lives he could write his message and who would go out from his presence to carry that message abroad" Before the twelve, he would have to find seven men and women to be the heart of his operation. They would have to start with 20 evangelism and when the day is over, it has to close out with evangelism. What will be their success?

giving a sinner man or woman the opportunity to say yes, or no to the salvation of Jesus Christ. There is no begging, just have a compassion for the souls of mankind.

The next foundational piece is finance. They will have to learn that giving 10% from the top and an offering is the only the beginning. The word teaches us to give joyfully, be a cheerful giver not grudgingly. Here is where the definition of stewardship slaps us in the face. it is the use of God given resources for accomplishing of God given goals. Most church members can very upset when talking about money management being a part of stewardship. They feel as if they can handle their own money. Yet, most of them would give considerably more to the church, if they were not in such debt.

A sacrificial gift must involve the beat of the heart. Sacrificial gift is what we have to do something else with. It is not waste money; neither is it throwing your money away. You make a decision that support the program's of the convention, and especially the district association. The amount that you offer to give must be an amount that you can continue to give as you have purposely said. It hurt, yes, but you believe that God will provide you with more than what you have.

The third level of giving is that what you want to give, but you do not have it to give. Example: John Henry wants desperately to give to the church's building fund program. He is presently tithing and giving an offering. He is making a sacrificial gift of fifty dollars a month, but he desire to give more. He shares with God that he want to give five thousand dollars a year from now to the church. He confesses that He do not have the financial resources, but if God provides him with the money he will give it. But if he does not, he will not have it to give.

Something bothered him; it was something that were not clear to him. He went over to his desk, withdrew his pipe and put it into his mouth. With a puzzle look he took out his tobacco pouch, opened it and with a concern look on his face, close it back. Took his pipe from his mouth and looked at it. Shaking his head he put the pipe in the ash tray. (For a moment he took on the life of a 45 year old man with three teen aged children. A family who \altogether earned 75 thousand dollars, would have a hard time giving and saving to support his family. He was not a mathematician. He knew enough to get by and because his job did not pay insurance or retirement; he had to save it from his weekly pay check.)

Rev. King sat down but he was uncomfortable in body, mind and spirit. He needed to figure out how this brother could pay his tithe and offering, the dues ministries and auxiliary of his local church he was involved with. His local brotherhood, Male choir dues, -city wide brotherhood donations, - district brotherhood dues, state brotherhood financial expectation, National Baptist Convention expectations financially. Annual days, and special church events. O yes the convention if he is involved as a brotherhood man. How can this brother come out ahead, put some money in saving and save for his retirement. He knew that he had to solve this young man's problem. He had to find a way to put him at spiritual ease, making him comfortable with his giving in all area's of stewardship. The men that he need to restore the district association need to feel an attitude of accomplishment.

They need to be aware that as they walk with God in his love, word, and commandments they will have more than enough for all of their responsibilities.

They must know and realize that their labor does not supply them the best that God have to offer. that their prosperity is coming from their obedience to an all mighty God. Their love for God and mankind wrapped up in a spirit of humanity, allows them to give above their means. He thought about the 8th chapter of 2 Corinthians "Out of the most severe trials, their overflowing joy and their extreme poverty welled up in rich generosity. They gave as much as they were able, and even beyond their ability. In verse 5 And they did not do as we expected, but they gave themselves first to the Lord and then to us I keeping with God's will. Verse 12 for if the willingness is there them the gift is acceptable according to what one has, not according to what he does not have." Giving, love and humanity should strike a pose in a believer's life and especially the lives of these few people who has been called out for the service of Jesus Christ.

There are three things that the association must teach those involved. This comes from the question that was asked two Sundays ago in women class #2 "If God is indeed our father, and he owns all of his creation, and especially the money. Then regardless how much money he gives away and share with others, He never has less than at the beginning, the amount that the father has is all, nor just today, but he will always own all the money in the world. If he then is to share with his children, he still own all the money in theworld." She stood there looking into the faces of people who were confused by her question or statement. Then she continues,

"Why must the Christian people who are all heirs to the kingdom, no one can be an heir except believers in Jesus Christ. With all that money he own, and we are his children, and yet we are poor. What is the problem, someone is falling down on their responsibility to God's little children."

King remembered her statement as if it was yesterday. If she could ask that question in a Sunday school class, there are more people than she is concerned about the lack of the Christian people in the financial arena of the church. He came to the conclusion that the district association must find a way to excite the people and motivate them. Three things that the association must drill into the hearts and conscious of those who lead. "They must give 10% from the top of their income or more and an offering, save five percent for the family, 1% for the needy, take the overflow and invest it in growth and income mutual stock fund. He knew that there will be people who disagree with him, but at least it is a start. He thought about the area where man does not have it to give, he wants to give a certain sum, he name that sum that he wants to give; if God provides the sum, he will give it, if he does not, he will not have it to give. The brother will give the sum he wants to give from the overflow, from blessings and promises of God.

There are three things that the association must teach those involved. This come from the question that was asked two Sundays ago in women class #2 "If God is indeed your father, and he owns all of His creation, and especially the money. Then regardless how much money he gives away or share with others, he never has less than at the beginning, the amount the father has is all, not just today, he will always own all the money in the world." She stood there looking into the faces of people who were confused by her question or statement.

Then she continued, "Why must the Christian people who are all heirs to the kingdom---no one can be an heir except believers in Jesus Christ.

With all that money he owes, and we are his children, and yet we are poor. What is the problem, someone is falling down on their responsibility to God's little children.

King remembered her statement as if it was yesterday. If she could ask that question in a Sunday school class, there are more people than she is concerned about the lack of the Christian people in finance arena of the church. He came to the conclusion that the district association must find a way to excite the [people and motivate them.

Three things that the association must drill into the heart and conscious of those who lead; "They mush give 10% or more, and an offering, save five percent for the family 1% for the needy, take the overflow and invest it in growth and income mutual fund stock. . He knew that there will be people who disagree with him, but at least it is a start. He thought about the area where man does not have it to, but desire to give a certain sum, when God bless him he can, and will give it. From this source of giving they will reap the overflow that only God can share with the believer from all that the father own.

A thought hit him between his heart and artistries and drove a stake between his eyes. He tried to remember where he had read the quote from a book that he had read recently. It reminded him that the men and women that he chooses, maybe he should say that he and God choosing will have to be special. When he thought about what he said, there were a long hesitation and on the inside he felt unsure of himself. His thoughts went back to Jesus Day and his mind picked upon the mind of Jesus calling the twelve.

Judging them by worldly standards the men Jesus chose had no special qualifications at all; they were not wealthy; they had no special social position; they had no special education; they were no trained theologian; they were not high ranking churchmen. They were twelve ordinary men. They had two purposes. He had called them to be with him and He called them to send them out. Jesus had equipped them with two things. First he gave them a message. It is said that men will always listen to a man with a message. Jesus gave them something to say. Then he gave them power. They were also to cast out demons. Because they complained with him something of his power was on their lives.

CHAPTER #3

God offers prayer for results

(Give therefore thy servant an understanding heart
to judge thy people that I may discern between
good and bad: for who is able to judge this thy so
great a people?") (1 King 3:9)

Rev. King could not even began to know what he was to do, how
he was to choose the right people, How to convince leadership who
had positions in the association. He had to find a way to turn their
minds in his direction. He tried praying more than once, and he
could not even bring Jesus into focus. Sitting there with his head
down, he thought about Dr. Franks, a good and trusted friend who
has pastured over 44 years at one church. He was well respected
through out the Christian world. When he talked, people young
and old would listen. They had respect for him over a lot of years,
they believed, that he believed God. He had a place that he went to
pray. When he wanted to talk to God, and he knew that God would
talk to him. When he went there God would be there waiting for
him. That was a few miles from here, about fifty miles from Dallas.

But he had a close friend, sometime he would go out to see her
and spend hours on hours. She would always let him know when it
was getting dark; it would be time to go. This is where he would go
when he needed help to share something difficult with God and he

needed an understanding that he understood in his practical life. When Dr. Franks was in a situation that boggled his mind, he went to see a saint that lived on farm road 1283, almost twenty miles down the road from any town. They never prayed together, but he would always return with the right thing to say and do. Therious did not know where this old Saint lived, all he knew that she was a Godly woman that people feared and respected. The best that he knew, she lived on farm road 1283. Dr. Franks would only say on occasion that the Lord met them there. There were people who followed him until he got to the old house, and then they would loose their way. Other people will swear that no one have lived there for years. The only movement is a man wearing stripped overalls would take a lantern and walk to the back of the property toward the river. It seems as if Dr. Franks was the only living soul that have ever seen her.

King was in trouble, the kind of trouble that the living God who lived in heaven, specialized in handling this kind of case. When King decided that he needed to communicate with her, there were no unction for him to go to that address. He stood there wondering; the forward spirit did not instruct him to leave the building. He thought about the people who have always said that she never existed, that no human had ever lived in that house. To this he recalled that Dr. Franks would drop his head and smile. While he was sitting there thinking with a confused mind, an angel of the Lord visited him. He spoke softly, "Servant, do not try to find her, she is available to you from here" The angel did not come close to him, but he could hear him clearly. Then he said, "Stand and look toward the East, raise your eyes until you see a low hung cloud just over the horizon, looking as if it was going to send, rain wind and hail. Down below the cloud look for a tree that has an old rickety swing, moving slowly in the breeze. You will not see her, but she is gently swinging in the in the wind. Tell her what you want".

He stood and looked toward the East, he saw nothing between there and the old house with a swing, slowly swinging through the breeze. It was as if he was standing across the road from the house.

There were a small dark Human body swinging under the shade tree. He could not tell who it was. The fear moved from him and a warm taste of confidence filled his chest. The reluctant feeling moved to the right of him and fell to the ground.

\Dr. King was housed with more problems that he can solve, and there is a selection of men and women out there some where that he must select from, Men and women that God had pre-qualified. Mature Christians who sometime did not know themselves what God wanted them to do. He stood there for a moment and a warm feeling fell over him. Without the presence of the Angel, confidence rose up in his chest and mind, and he spoke toward the East as if he was looking in the face of a friendly person. Then he spoke, "I have a task that has weighed me down to my knees, but on my knees I cannot get a prayer through to my father. You and I have a friend in presence, he has passed on but he left your address in a mental vault, that I have the key. I need your help and of all the people that I can think of, you are the person that I desperately need. I don't know how to approach you, and I don't know what to say, so please forgive me if I say the wrong thing.

Rev. King could see the swing slowly moving in the breeze and sitting in the swing was a small figure that he could not make out. He assumed that it was the old saint that lived by the old farm road that led to nowhere. He finally got the courage to speak; You know more about what I want than I do. It was then that he heard a soft voice spoken with authority. "You are where you are supposed to be, anywhere else you would be out of place.

"I talked to my friends in heaven, they told me that you would be coming" by. Rev. King did not know where he was, he was in a mental state that should have confused him, but it did not. It was as if something warm had settled down over him, and then he spoke.

"Pray to my father that he would give me the prayer that he will accept from me to pray to him for this matter. When he has given me the prayer, I will bow on humble knees and pray the prayer that he has given me. I will receive an answer from him, when I pray the prayer that he has given me to pray. If he gives me the proper prayer to pray to him, I know that He hears me. If I know that He hears me, whatever I ask, we know that we have the petition that we have asked of him. My asking will be his will, because it will be his prayer that we are praying. The prayer that will get results. It is His will. He would not give me a prayer that would not get results from a mighty God. . "Will you pray to the father for me, ask him if he will give me the prayer to he wants me to pray to him for this situation at hand. I do not know how to pray this special prayer. If he give me the prayer to pray, I am sure that I will be successful in reaching him.

And if I reach him, I know he will hear my prayer. I cannot reach him, but I know you can, and I believe that through you He will.

Therious King knees went limp and he cried out to God. There before him stood the son of God sitting at the right hand of the father. He could not see his savior eyes, for both the father and the son was looking in his direction. After he had gotten through speaking, the son turned and looked at the father, and the father nodded yes to his son. When the son looked back at King, they were gone. He felt in his heart that God was going to be with him all the way. He found himself upon his knees weeping and praising God. He was not sure what God had given him, but he knew that it was enough to get him home.

Rev. King knew that God had given him a vision, a plan and a goal, yes; he had given him a message. It was not presently clear, how he would accomplish the mission, but he had the vision. He had received the message that he had a hard time believing himself. The message was for those who have received his son Jesus Christ as their personal savior, have repented of their sin and ask God to forgive them of their disobedience; he would share with them a love that only he could give. The Holy Spirit that would dwell within them would give them the power to accomplish the mission. In the book of Mark 16: 17-18 NIV. "And these signs will accompany those who believe: In my name they will drive out demons; they will speak in new tongues; they will pick up snakes with their hands; and when they drink deadly poison, it will not hurt them at all; they will place their hands on sick people, and they will get well."

Therious knew that he did not have the slightest idea how he was going to accomplish this with the men and women he had never seen. The same message that Jesus gave to his disciples, is the same message that he must give to those who will be following him. Jesus had all power, there weren't anything that he did not know. Those who followed him walked in the foot step of the all mighty God who had all power. Rev. King wanted to throw up his hands, there was too much that he did not know coming at him at the same time. The time that he had to train the men and women that he had not chosen yet was approximately eight months. He had to show the State convention that he could do the job. Bringing 10 churches back into the Cap/Rock would go a long ways to prove that he had the right people and the right message. It was necessary that the evidence of progress Would be in place before October of the following year.

This being November 2015\There is no doubt that this journey will be a difficult one, but at the end, a resting place, the journey is well worth the trip. He thought about the inner conflict that each person must over come, conflict they were not aware of. In some a mysterious conflict, over looked by the conscious mind, but is renewed by the subconscious mind, which from time to time is the driving force of a lifted human being. We are talking about people who never knew that there is an enemy fighting them in their own mind. It is there to create conflict, doubt, fear and unbelief in an area of your mind that has been left empty or void of God's word. A place that ordinary prayer may not touch, may not know to understand, but allows Satan space to occupy the soul until the spirit of God come and drives him out.

Let us look at this a little further, a block that keep us from getting our requested promises and blessings may come from a source that we least expect to see or feel. David A Seaman had this to say about a blockage to the abundant life. "That there is another realm of problems, which require a special kind of prayer and a deeper level of healing by the spirit. Some where between our sins on one hand and our sickness, on the other, lays an area the scripture calls, "Infirmities"?

David went on to say, " Just a few minutes beneath the protective bark, the concealing, protective mask, are the recording rings of our lives ... ... as when a little boy rushes down stairs one Christmas dawn and discovered in his Christmas stocking a dirty old rock, put there to punish him for some trivial boyhood naughtiness. This scar has eaten away in him, causing all kinds of interpersonal difficulties." Then he went on to say, "In the rings of our thoughts and emotion, the record is there; the memories and emotions; the memories are recorded and all are alive. And they directly and deeply affect our concept, our feelings, and our relationship. They affect the way that we look at life, and God, at others and at ourselves." It is these hidden problems that can cause us not to believe that God can do what he promised he would do. With problems long forgotten from the outer layer pokes up his head because of something that uncovers him, we let this problem clog up our request to God. It interferes with our request when we go beyond our everyday desire to receive.

Rev. King Went over next to the door, there were a cabinet that no one entered but himself. He opened the little lock, looked at the contents of the cabinet, then his watch, it was a little past 2 o'clock in the morning.

He knew that Monday morning was coming soon and he needed to get some things settled in his mind. He was not sure if the number would be twelve or seven. Yes, he said to himself it will be both, there will be seven, then twelve. But where in the world would he get the man and women that met the qualification. When he did not know what the qualification really was. Maybe that was not exactly true, they had to be Christians who had faith in Jesus Christ and believed in the word of God. That would mean that they are obedient to the will of God and keeper of the word of God.

The criteria for each person would have to be the same. But then how could that be, no two persons are the same. He was getting a little confused, not angry but frustrated because he could not figure it our in his mind. He was not exactly sure how this was going to come out. He thought about praying, but that would come when he had some idea what he was doing. His knowing for sure, even with God's direction would be difficult.

For he had to figure in his own doubts and fears. He came to the conclusion that he would choose them one at a time and wait on God to put his stamp on each one of them. He would have to be patient and prayful as Jesus was on the Mt. of Olives before his death. He thought about those words, he thought about the prayer and the intensity of the request of Jesus. He wondered how it would change his life style in this process of things. For he has a wife-he has a pastors wife, with pastors kids. Set then down in front of God and they will understand. He thought about the angel from heaven that came down to assist Jesus, and then he prayed more earnestly.

Luke 22:39-He was not sure how he was going to do that. He knew that if he tried God would assist him in his request. He needed men and women who was sold out to the kingdom of heaven, at all cost.

He turned and looked at a picture on the wall, it was an old man they call poppa. Life had ceased from his soul here on earth, but his influence was spreading by the account of the need of fellow preachers. He remembered the words of the old man a few years ago. They were attending a state convention. He said, "If you are going to build a church or anything about a building that house baptize believers. Build it on men. They may be hard to teach, difficult to learn, but the effort is well worth the labor in a long run. Build men even if they are not Aware of what God want them to do.

Brothers, teach them, live the life in front of them. If you do wrong, which you should not do, don't let them know of your disobedience.

Make it an effort to teach them the hard truth, even when it hurts. Sharing the gospel in such a way that the unsaved can make the decision to accept the message or reject."

The old pastor would clear his throat, and look out into

nothingness. He would then quote Mark 10:17-22;niv "----a man ran up to Jesus and fell on his knees before him, "Good teacher, what must I do to inherit eternal life?" "Why do you call me good?" Jesus answered. "No one is good--except God alone. You know the commandments; So not murder, do not commit adultery, do not steal, do not give false testimony, do not defraud, honor your father and mother." "Teacher "he declared all these I have kept since I was a boy." Jesus looked at him and loved him. One thing you liked," he said, "Go sell everything you have and give it to the poor.

and you will have treasures in heaven. Then come, follow me" ..." At this the man's face fell. He went away sad, because he had great wealth. (NIV). The old man would look at you. Never soften the blow of salvation; it is a hard reality that one must absorb. When you are sharing the gospel, tell the truth, anything less than the truth is unfair to God. It may not sound good, and it may turn the person away, but you must tell the truth.

The modern church has been walking away from the way of God for a long time. He and other pastors have witnessed the slow decline of the good news for a few years. Witnessing, evangelistic teams that go out and knock on door and talk to people in their yard are a thing of the past. The church have failed to come together as a body of baptized believers under the power and direction of an all mighty God. 80% of members who go to church has little or no understanding of sharing the gospel of Jesus Christ. The leaders of the church, Pastor, Deacons, Trustees and bible teachers, has made a conscious decision not to be obedient to Gods word. Satan has fooled them, in believing that sharing His word is not important, just share as you go, because there will always be some one sharing if you do not.

Therious King went to his seat behind the desk; putting his feet on the desk, he laid back in his recliner, put the old man's picture face down on his chest, closed his eyes and asked God to give him some direction. He was aware that God had just departed his company. But his soul remained connected, or----was it. O Yes he could ask for directions, but he would have to wait unto morning to see his way. The message, is God's knowledge and information, it is solid and good, what is to be accomplished is God's will, the choosing of the men and women still was not clear. But there were one thing that was clear; Church people had forgotten who God was. They knew his name, they read about him in the Bible, they talked about how good he is, and how much power that he had.

But when it came down to the final straw, they had forgotten who Christ is. Matthew 28:19-20 nivcame to mind, "Go yea therefore, and teach all nations, Baptizing them in the name of the father, and the son, and off the Holy Ghost: Teaching them to observe all things whatsoever I have commanded you; and lo I am with you always, even unto the end of the world" He found himself in a dimly lighted room with statures of other God's, they were trying to speak to him, but a light came into the room and stood him in the light of the room. He then could not see the idle god's, but he realized it was an angel from heaven to assist him in his desire to please God. The voice that came from over the bright light that stood in the corner seem to speak to him. He forgets that God is a God of wrath, and anger when his people refuse to be obedient to his word.

CHAPTER #4

Following away of the church

(As it is written, how beautiful are the feet of them
that preach the gospel of peace and bring glad tiding
of good things.) (Rom. 10:15)

Why, the question kept coming back to him? Why have the church
left the straight and narrow for a broad road that leads to destruction.
Why should God's people slide back into disobedience when the
road is so clear? What about life that is temporary at best. Life lived
that we are certain that it will end with the grave. No! life does not
end with the grave; it began at the entrance of the grave. Why is a
little pleasure of the flesh, a little sin that seem to be no harm, so
powerful in the life of the church? How does the believer of our faith
in Jesus Christ allow the slipping away of our faith in Jesus Christ?
How can we turn our back on him when he never turn his back on
us? How can we replace those hot, soul felt brawny tears of the love
of God, for a cold hurry up and move on Amen.

The only thing that he could come up with is that they have
forgotten him. But how have they forgotten their Lord and savior
who promises them eternal life if they remain faithful. They
attend church every week, read their bibles and pray, believing that
God hears and answers their prayers. But the unforgiving sin of
disobedience to God hang on. Here lies the danger of every believers,

if we don't stay faithful to the word of God, we will move slowly, ever so slowly from God; and at the same time not know what is happening to our soul. The sin of disobedience in the face of God; when he has commanded us to a task; or in this case a command to keep the gospel alive. The sin of disobedience is the face of God when he has commanded us to a task; or in this case a command to keep the gospel alive. Only a believer can keep the gospel alive, no one else have the story, no one have the experience, and no one else have walked with God. No one else surrender their lives to a person that cannot be seen, but have accepted him in faith. No one have the testimony to share the goodness and powerful of God except a believer Then walk away from the only hope that they have.

Before the father's Son could go back home to be with his father: He left a command that was a covenant agreement between the Father, Son, and believers. The command is the word from God for his people to do a certain thing. This certain thing was to share the word of God for salvation. . Failure to do what he has commanded, results in sin. The covenant agreement he made was with those who loved him, a covenant that he signed in his own blood. Braking of this covenant required repentance, asking forgiveness will not be received until true repentance have been agree upon between the father, Son and the believer. Praying to God to forgive you for all of your sins, does not include the sin of disobedience of sharing the word of God. Repenting that one has sin, because he has not obeyed God's word, he confessed it and repent. That mean that he will stop not doing what God has commanded us to do. You can see how that un-repented sin stack upon a believer until he cannot carry the heavy load any longer. His un-repented sin stacks so high until God cannot answer their prayers without repentance. Why should one repent when he is sure that heaven is his home. And since the believer is comfortable with his life style, he believes that a loving God is full of mercy and grace would not allow him two suffer the end results if he does not stop sinning.

Sure he said to himself I am good for life.

The fact and the truth remain; however close they once were not even God will not stop you from your own will. He can yes, he has the power. When a believer walks away it is to his own will.

It hurt Jesus, because it crucifies him again.?H-6:4. How is that believer, if he still remain a believer get back into a right relationship with the father. When that believer come to himself; repent of his sin of not sharing the Gospel that God had commanded him to do, and start sharing it with compassion for the soul of man. It is not easy, for he thinks that he is in good relationship with God. He has volunteered to accept some of Satan's direction in his life without knowing what he is doing. There are two spirits, God almighty, and Satan angry with Jesus for throwing him out of heaven. It is his job to destroy you or temp you to sin, which in a long run will destroy you.

What has happen to believers that cause them to walk away from God in sharing the good news. Surely we know that God is not please with our walk. How can he be; when sharing the good news is the only way to spread the gospel to all the world. All believers, mature Christians and baby Christian are needed to carry the word. King shook his head and realized that he is in over his head. If he could not get men, some called to preach the gospel, others have their qualification embedded in his word; if he cannot get them to share the gospel with compassion for the soul, he would not be successful with a project he would give his right arm to be a part of. His fear now is that at the job ahead, getting deeper into what has to happen, is covering him in his inability to grasp it all.

He knew he had to figure out why the church has walked away from sharing the good news. He knew that they had forgotten who he was. But how to share with them in such a way they would realize their mistake, turn around and with the love of God be obedient to his word. As he sat there puzzled not knowing for sure what he has to do. One of the seven young men that had crossed over in front of him to the right, reappeared. He looked to be eighty years old, but Barnes recognized him as one of the young men. His skin was drawn, had not had a haircut or a shave in months, his eyes seem to be void of sleep, yet they were strong with a message.

The vision that God was bringing Rev. King into the path of this young, old man was filled with awe. It did not seem to be a place at all, it was a meeting place below the third heaven, where God had come down to meet him. Though God came down, he was moved up out of the rhyme and this became their meeting place. King did not see God but he knew that he was there. There were no fear, no doubt, no goals, just a meeting place to clear the air for an assignment that he did not know that God had anything to do with. He wanted to feel surprise, but he could not get that surprise feeling. The atmosphere was so calm, he was in a place, but it did nor seem to be a place, except maybe one that God had set aside for this purpose.

Then he found out that the young, old man had escorted him to this place; out of the rhyme of fleshy desires. Out into the space of time where sin was not welcome. God had to give humans beings a special invitation, and then send a escort for his arrival and departure. Sometime the departure was so sudden the person did not know that they had ever been there.

Rev. King did not know if he was standing or sitting. He heard what he thought was the voice of the old man, but he did not see him. "The task that you have agreed to, is not man to give, it belong to my father. They believe that you will fail, but don't worry, I am beside you. It will not be easy to follow my instructions, but you can do it."

There seem to have been a silence forever, when he spoke it was not in words, he did not hear a single word after the silence had passed. He came to him in an unction, a heavenly voice that a man with sin could not understand. Rev. King knew that he had to get all of the information now because he may never go this way again. The unction impressed upon his mind and heart that, there were a group of words that he had to listen for; those words were, "IS ALL WELL WITH YOUR SOUL." Remember he said, all who use these words will not be a candidate for service. When you talk to them you will know. But remember you cannot allow yourself to enter into a state of un-repented sin. I will warn you in the spirit and in God's word. 1 Corinthians 10:13 NIV. "No temptation has seized except what is common to man. And God is faithful, he will not let you be tempted beyond what you can bear. But when you are tempted, he will also provide a way out so that you can stand up under it. "Do not close your eyes to sleep if you even think that there is something negative between us; until you know that nothing exist.

Get your people to agree that it is a sin not to share the Gospel of Jesus Christ. Because the only way for the gospel to spread into all the world, every believer has to do his share is sharing the good news. If we refuse to obey God in one area, his blessings and promises will cease to be effective. The church cannot call God father, Lord of their lives, the head of their lives when they are intentionally disobedient.

How can God keep them through the night, protect them, watch over them, while they sleep in disobedience. Fear should come upon every believer who lie down with un-repented sin in their lives. Whichever one does not believe it is necessary to be obedient to God's word; dismiss him with love.

Rev. King found himself a little dizzy, the old folks says that his head was swimming and it did not clear until he sat down. As long as his eyes were open he was dizzy, but when he shut his eyes it seem to disappear.

When he was not dizzy, he did not feel comfortable. It was then that he realized that the closing of the eyes was about him. He could see three (topics) standing off as if they had legs. He recognized them as a problem into days church's.

The content of their soul was not a stranger to the church, but it was their obedience that he knew was missing. Of the three sharing the good news one was in red, the other two was in green. There were no haziness about them, they were clear. Now the words appeared before him in large bright letters dripping in red blood. Not running blood just drips here and there.

He began to read the words that seem to pass in front of him.- "Evangelism is more than leading the unsaved to Christ; it is an attitude and mindset to please God at all cost. There are three scriptures that set the foundation of the suffering and death of Jesus Christ. Luke 22:39- 44. When it became black dark all over the world. and Luke 14:25-30. Matthew 26:36-46 The cost is sometime so great that we walk away from him, but not before we convince ourselves that we do not need him or there is no life after death. These scriptures are the driving force, which experienced with his resurrection.

This attitude change is the results of a movement in the mind that wakes up the physical, sociological, and spiritual energy power in action. Our response to the tremendous awakening power drives our creative energy to unconsciously explode into action that we have created ourselves. It is said that if nothing moves, nothing will happen. If the conscious never wakes up, there will be no attitude.

When this functional action has searched and found direction, you are the only one who has the power to instruct our awakening energy into a mindset of possible accomplishments. Once your mindset has taken control of our attitude we can then accomplish our desired goals.

Many times a mindset change is needed to change our feeling and knowledge of things we have seen, touched or heard". Rev. King could not stop the words from going across in the front of him. He did not understand them all, they were not clear to him. He was becoming a little frustrated-then all of a sudden, he was relaxed and at peace with himself.

It looks like the words were waiting for him without him knowing, it being aware. They` said, "When the right mindset and attitude have been inserted into place these young men and women will answer the age-old question: Do we see an ever expanding company of dedicated men reaching the world with the gospel as a result of this ministry? Oh, yes we are busy in church trying to work one program of evangelism, after another cannot be denied. But are we accomplishing our objective."

The words kept coming, "evangelism should be an effort to see controlling principals governing the moment of the master in the hope that our own labors might be conformed to a similar pattern. These young men should not be as concerned about Jesus in personal or mass evangelism. Rather they should know the principals underlying His ministry--principals which determines his methods. If you choose, one could call this attitude Jesus' strategy of evangelism". Rev. King were waiting on the words to stop flowing, but that was not to be. They kept on coming.

Look at Matthew 28:19-20niv: 'Go ye therefore, and teach all nations, baptizing them in the name of the father, and of the son, and of the Holy Ghost. Teaching them to observe all things whatsoever I have commanded you: and, low I am with you always, even unto the end of the world" Mark 16:15-18niv Open up God's direction to a better understanding. Look especially at verse 17 and 18, "And these signs shall follow them that believe; in my name they shall cast our devils; they shall speak with new tongues; They shall take up; and if they drink any deadly thing, it shall not hurt them; they shall lay hands on the sick, and they shall recover." In Luke's writing, Acts 1:8; He gives considerably more information, in fewer words. "But ye shall receive power, after the Holy Ghost has come upon you. And ye shall be witnesses unto to men both in Jerusalem, and Judea, and in Samaria, and unto the utmost parts of the earth." look how God give his own people direction that they may be obedient and faithful to him. Man was never created for any other purpose than to be obedient to the father.

Rev. King felt a moment of relief, but it was not to be enjoyed. It was a message to him personally, it was about a weakness that he was not fully aware of. He could feel his father looking at him, but the look was not a friendly look, it was stern, a look that shouted out in silence.

You have a spirit that is foreign to your father, he is displeased that it abides in the same place where the spirit of God resides.(He noticed that God never blinks his eyes, he never drop his head, and he never looks in another direction. The silence shout informed him that the craving to be someone special, far above everyone else. This spirit would have to go, and be replaced by the spirit of a little child who is obedient to his father. At that moment he realized that total surrender was the spirit that he needed from the Lord. It was strange for him to believe that anyone could turn their selves over to God and walk in the light of the fathers direction. He realized that saying that he was not perfect with a smile, had to go. For now he knew that perfect did not mean sinless, it mean being obedient to God and the spirit that dwell within himself. He knew then that what God wanted from him, was something that he had never gave before. Saved yes, total surrender, never before. But to accomplish this task----a task that should have been accomplished a long time ago. Then he thought that, long time ago was in the past. And though he was a young man he had more time behind him then he had in front of him. He felt himself turning himself over to the guidance of an almighty God.

He felt the power of the Lord coming upon him as it never have done before. When he became aware of himself, the writing had started to move again. Our days of trifling are running out. The evangelistic programs of the church has bogged down on nearly every front. The great commission thrust of the Gospel into new frontier has largely lost its power. The world and its ways are coming more into the church, than the church is sharing with the world.

The church has failed at the responsibility of building men for the mission. You now have that responsibility to train these souls, even though they are entrenched in their ways, and from time to time listen to Satan direction. It is an awesome responsibility that man alone cannot do; but with God all things are possible. There is a lot of talk in church about evangelism and Christian nurture, but little concern for personal association when it comes evident that such work involves the sacrifice of personal indulgence.

No one should take on the challenge of evangelism unless he is ready to make a commitment to the process of evangelism.

There is a condition and a cost to follow Jesus. No money need to change hands, but a sacrifice is a must that God requires. These men and women must make up his or her mind before the journey that this responsibility is wrapped God's word. The father more than anyone else want the believer to succeed. Every believer should take up the challenge of sharing the Gospel.

Rev. King took a small stick of candy from his pencil case on the desk, slowly removing the peeling away. Crumbed it up in his hand and threw it into the trash can. It was then that he knew that this journey would be almost a secret. No one would talk about it in the meetings, at the state level, national level or district level, to accomplish this task. He knew now that this task would not bring fame and recognition. With all honesty for a few minutes he was disappointed, then he realized that God was in his presence and looking at him. He apologized underneath his breath and looked in the direction that the words had been coming at him quicker than he could understand them.

He knew that God had (WOULD)strengthen him for the task and the journey. For a moment the peppermint stick had become a little bitter, bitter enough to get his attention. (MEANING)(The sweet peppermint stick represents the information that he is receiving is true to him, and he relaxes in his comfort zone. But when the story became uncomfortable-in an area where he might have been guilty or at least did not understand.) He had heard this story that seem to be directed to him and his followers: A young man wanting to impress his lady to be, he ran up to an old renowned college professor on a collage campus by the sea side.. "Good master", he said, "I want to be a brilliant teacher like you. I want to have the knowledge and wisdom that you have," The old teacher stopped him, hesitated for a while then asked him again what he wanted. The young man repeated his question in the same words. The teacher, seeing that the young man was serious, but not aware of what lay ahead of him., said, "come" he said to the young man. "Come with me to the water of the sea." The young man followed him while his lady waited on the seashore. They went out about five feet and then faced each other. He asked him again, and again he got the same answer. He dipped the young man underneath the water, and after a while he let him up. He again asked the same question as what he wanted. And again he gave him the same answer.

He took the young man beneath the surface of the water three times and three times asked him the same question. And all three times he got the same answer. Finally he dipped the young man underneath the water until he could feel the young man scuffling for his life. Quickly he bought him to the top and then asked him what he wanted. The young man trying to catch his breath, said, "air" The old college professor said to him "When you want to be a teacher like I am, as bad as you want air you can have it." Commitment is the engine that drives the train, and without it the train goes nowhere.

Commitment and influence must stand head and shoulders above the individual person.

Rev. King is again feeling a little uncomfortable and the candy has become so bitter that he takes it from his mouth. By now he is aware that something distasteful is coming up next.. The candy falls from his hand and brakes into three pieces. There on the floor it rest side by side, and a closer look find that the peppermint in the candy have been taken away and has dripped to the floor. (Kings way of life in this area have not been total righteous, he find himself guilty of disobedience.) The candy is without any use. But the roaring of the river overflows and washes the peppermint back on the un-sweet sticks of candy. He looks up and see a familiar sight, it is words that he have been trying to teach his people. But his teaching has fallen on death ears and the church has continued to fall apart. But again the words began to move forward.

"The rites of passage by which people become members of religious communities are well known. The rite of passage by which people leave the 'tipping phenomenon' remains unexplored. The church leadership finds in-active-drop-outs to be an interesting subject, but they can't pull the trigger on action. The church membership is frustrated with leadership of the church because they seem not to care about the direction that God has given the church concerning in-active members. God is concern about in-active members that take the time to place their membership, as the churches has done with the district association and then walked away. Your job is to treat the churches who once was a part of your group as in-active-dropouts. You need to bring them back to the foe. Speak with them with compassion. It is a sure thing that they have been hurt, or they misunderstood what God's intention was for their lives. Remember the scripture that says,

(When you speak, you should do it as one speaking the very words of God.

And when you serve, you should do it with the strength God provides, so that in all things God may be praised through Jesus Christ. To the father be the glory and the power forever.)Never forget that winnings souls and bringing wayward churches to the district, is never easy. Because you want to bring them back with compassion. They are hurt and they are injured, many feel as if they are not wanted and others feel as if they are wanted for what the district can get out of them. Never forget that the district is run by preachers, and messenger when all is said and done, most of the money fall to them. All of the authority, instructions and control is in the hand of preachers. Do not forget that many pastors talk negatively about their membership, they call them crazy, ignorant and stupid, and then they laugh at them with other pastors. Keep in mind that the reason why some churches have walked away is that they have a heart, soul and spirit that have been mashed and stomped on by preachers. Some churches has learned to hate people who run these organizations, some have become so bitter until revenge is the only comfort that they search for.

(The peppermint stick voluntary falls from his lips again and while it is falling, it breaks into three falling parts. When it hit the floor it breaks up into the shape of a mini sand dome. On the other side of the sand dome, facing east, strolls a slick black Raven, he wasn't looking at King, he was observing him. The Raven did not pay any attention to the black buzzard that flew in unwanted and landed on a brown dead tree limb, he bobbled a couple of tines to get his balance, then he started to observe Rev. King. The rabbit, yes the rabbit looked toward Rev. King and then turned and ran toward the sea. The rabbit had only three legs, but his stroke was smooth, his gate like a horse in stride. But he knew that he would never reach the ocean. He was happy to have a silk smooth silk stride. King was confused. King seem to always be confused, for the raven represent peace and tranquility, the buzzard-death and trouble, the rabbit the mystery that has not been unveiled. Then a clap of thunder raised his head and declared his superiority, he held back the lightening, untilTherious could calm himself. This understanding put the situation into a far distant sight. All he had heard and seen need not come together tonight, God is going to give him time. But he himself stood as a man and the shaking of the house brought Rev. Kings to his feet. The place where the writing had been was blank, looking as if it was waiting to be occupied.

But instead a voice of unction, as mellow and soothing to the mind, spirit, and soul. Rev. King needed this feeling because he had been under a tremendous strain to understand what was going on.

The unction came directly from the bible, he recognized it as being 1 Timothy chapter #3,(living bible) Beginning with verse 1. The unction said, "It is a true saying that if a man wants to be a pastor he has a good ambition. For a pastor must be a good man whose life cannot be spoken against. He must have only one woman, and he must be hard working and thoughtful, orderly,, and full of deeds. He must enjoy having guest in his house. And must be a good Bible teacher. He must not be a drinker or quarrelsome, but he must be gentle and kind, and not be one who loves money. He must have a well behaved family, with children who obey quickly and Quietly. For if a man cannot make his own little family behave, how can he help the whole church.? The pastor must not be a new Christian, \because he might be proud of being chosen so soon, and pride comes with a fall. (Satan's downfall is an example) Also he must be well spoken of by people outside the church-those who aren't Christian-so that Satan can't trap him with many accusation, and leave him without freedom to lead the flock."

The deacons that you are going to use. "The deacon must be the same sort of good, steady men as the pastor. They must not be heavy drinkers and must not be greedy for money. They must be earnest, wholehearted followers of Christ who is the hidden source of faith. Before they are asked to be deacons they should be given other jobs in the church as a test of their character and ability, and if they do well, then they may be chosen as deacons. There wives must be thoughtful, not heavy drinkers, not gossipers, but faithful in everything they do. Deacons should have only one wife, and they should have happy, obedient families. Those who do well as deacons will be well rewarded both by respect from others and also by developing their own confidence and bold trust in the Lord."

That came directly from God, he had been given his marching orders, his instructions came directly from the father himself. He know without a word or without a doubt that God wanted him to find the men and women and teach them His way. But before he (Walked out to the road to start his journey)reached out toward his journey, he, himself would have to master the words of his heavenly father, before he looked out toward the dusty road that lead to success; a rocky and treacherous road that cause the feet to develop coins underneath as well as on top of the toes. But the mind, body and soul must keep leaning forward. Their journey on this rocky road is to fine people to drive others home, what must be done in the task before him? Only now he had began to see that the journey ahead of him, was more than what he himself could handle. He knew it was difficult from the outset, but now from within, even with Gods help, it was going to be a difficult task. But then God specializes in human impossibilities. He must be able to guide the hand of these disciples. Not only must he believe but he must act out his belief.

CHAPTER #5

Without challenge there is no faith

(Let your speech be always with grace, seasoned
with salt, that you may know how ye ought to
answer every man.) (Col. 4:6)

He now realized that the task is a challenge even at the edge of the
second heaven. A place that he has never been before. (And to return
while taking this journey is beyond his comprehension.) It's kind
of like the pencil rocking at the end of the desk, it was sharpen on
both sides, and then sharpen in the middle on both sides. (What he
knows about the financial resources of mankind, is puzzling to him,
because his life did not live out Gods internal word. He lived in an
area of comfort, not sacrifice or suffering for the cause of Christ. The
confusion, the puzzling, and yes, the doubt and fear that sometime
loomed too large to comprehend, will cause Rev. King to repeat
himself, it is more of a mumbling and whinning. He finds himself
repeating things that he has said, he repeat them for clarification,
and clarity, and then he looks un-intelligent for a moment, then it
passes away.

The pencil began to write while it lay flat ways on the table. This
is an impossible feat, no one writes with a flat pen, or pencil, it just
can't be done; but then again the words were coming from the led
of the pen. "Every disciple must live the true meaning of the word of

God. The giving disciples must flourish in his finance, and it must be seen in the community of each person that you choose. People in general no longer give to the church or district organization simply because it is the organization of choice. The district association must prove it is worthy of the donation through the mark it leaves on the world. The district association have failed the principals of God. Thereby they have failed the people who have and do look to them for leadership in this area. The association have no problem teaching them tithe and offering; but they have a problem teaching them how to become financial independent through their giving.

They have a problem sharing with the people how to set the mind-set, the motive and the attitude of a man who seeks the best that God has to offer.

You must remember that each brother or sister have already paid their tithes and offerings to the church of their choice, and has given on their annual days and anniversary. Now you ask them to give over an eight of what they have in their pockets to the association, in time And human resources, for this, what does God promise he will do for them? Can you teach them how to get the best that God has to offer. That will be a steward's blessings in abundance. You may not have believed it or lived it in the past,. but you must in the future. The pencil turned, The pencil spinning around on its side, the side that it was writing with. The writing began to sound as if a man is talking to another man. Somehow the heavenly atmosphere has moved from heaven to a brook standing alone at the river's edge. It is like a father who is talking to his son. The son is not allowed to talk, just listen. The wind that blew around them took a deep breath and then began to talk. There are certain kind of men you should not choose from, not even to train for this work. Here we will not allow you to make a mistake.

"Jude 1:12-16, 18.nivThese men are blemishes at your love feast, eating with you without the slightest qualm--shepherds who feed only themselves. They are clouds without rain, blown along by the wind; autumn trees, without fruit and uprooted--twice dead. They are wild waves of the sea, forming up their shame; wandering stars, for whom blackest darkness has been reserved forever.

Enoch, the seventh from Adam, prophesied about these men: 'See the lord is coming with thousands upon thousands of his holy ones. To judge everyone, and to convict all the ungodly of all the ungodly acts they have done in the ungodly way, and of all the harsh words un- godly sinners have spoken against him. These men are grumblers and fault finders; they follow their own evil desires; they boast about themselves and flatter others for their own advantage." These kind of men should not be chosen. Your flesh may make a mistake, but I will be on your left shoulder. If you accept this assignment, and you have, when it is all over you will know what Jesus Christ went through here on earth.

The men that you choose will share the good news, they will share the news with compassion for the love of souls. Their desire and motive is to show leadership in the area of financial resources. And to develop a relationship with God, with the house hold of faith and his creation. They will be stewards in the truest sense of the word., steward's in the family of an all mighty God.

Where the abundance of all financial resources belong to God; Whatever day God shares some of his wealth with believers, it will not take away from how much he own. However much he gives, he still own it all.

you contact him, he still own all the money in the world. He will never give all His money away, because those who receive it will not live on this earth forever. They cannot take it with them; wherever they go, they will have to leave it behind. What is the reason for God's ownership. So faithful servants can use his abundance while they are on earth; they are called stewards. What then is a steward, an old man who could barely speak said that "The steward is God's responsible reprehensive and manager of all creation.' Grand mother Caroline says that steward is one who manages another person's property. He is not an owner who has rights; he is a manager who has responsibilities. My dad God bless his soul, said " Stewardship is the use of God given resources for accomplishing of God given goals."

The young man must believe that stewardship is an act of worship which mean that we should recognize that God is the owner of all things, and keeping his objectives, best interests and glorification in mind should be all we do. When we give a gift to ministry efforts, it is our way of thinking him for his love and generosity shown to us. We are called to worship him by using every breath and every ounce of energy we possess, that is to live our lives as a worship performance, which is the act of giving. That is another avenue for expressing poor humility and love for Him. One cannot have the mind of giving and not reap the blessings it affords.

We must be careful here; DEBT! This rolling rag weed of physical trouble ushers in the (valley of human struggle). Without a doubt debt is the largest road block a Christian have to go through, to achieve financial independence. Debt is a harsh reality that hides itself beneath emotions, misunderstanding, and poor teaching in the church, with the possible exception of life insurance and Tithing.

A. Debt is not a sin! The Bible discourages the use of debt, but it does not prohibit it.

B. Debt is never the real problem; it is only symptomatic of the real problem-greed, self-indulgence, impatience, fear, poor self-image, lack of self-worth, lack of self of self-discipline, and perhaps many others.

C. Debt can be defined in many ways. Let us define debt as money owed to anyone for anything. Others has recorded it, as money owed on the purchase of a depreciating item.

With our definition there are five kinds of debt: credit card debt, consumer debt, mortgage debt, investment debt, and business debt. We must never forget that debt is a symptom of much deeper problems, watch this- it keep us from experiencing God's best for us.

Debt will be a study in the association. It is advised that all churches will bind together with stewardship, and will use teachers from the association to share the concept of debt. We must know how dangerous debt is in the hindrance of our financial independence.

Let us touch on five things, and then we are going to move on. Understanding Biblical principals. This understanding only occurs when you have made that commitment to know God's will for your financial life.

2. Adopt a non-consumptive lifestyle. Live simply, frugally, make saving a priority to enable you to reach the financial goals God sets before you.
3. Avoid the use of debt. As we have seen, nothing is more destructive to your financial health than debt.
4. Keep your liquidity high. The first step in investing is to make sure you have adequate emergency funds (liquid assets) you can use quickly.
5. Long term goals. If you aim at nothing, you will hit everything.

NOTE: God's simple but radical financial principals can lead to solid stewardship and financial freedom. Proverbs 21:5, The plans of God lead surely to plenty, but those of everyone who is hasty, surely to poverty. Proverbs 30:25; Proverbs 6:6-8.

Setting goals carefully and following them diligently brings rewarding benefits to God's steward.

The men and women that you choose for this task must have an understanding, a understanding so deep that you can wake them at 3 A.M.

And half sleep, they can tell you the concept of Debt, the meaning of ten percent giving from the top, How our faithfulness to God can make us prosperous, and how our compassion for souls will turn the world in the kingdom direction

The men that is choose must speak to God concerning the three ways of giving, that you will teach those you have chosen.? Son listen to me carefully, YOU MUST TEACH, this have to be the hardest teaching job that you have ever done. They must understand that the church is the most cash intensive organization in the world. No other organization can use up all the money that they receive as a church or association.

As a matter of fact, the reason for securing sufficient funds for a church or association is for the purpose of funding ministry needs and every day activity.

What is it that these people must grasp if they are to lead the people where they worship? For them to understand their responsibility in the area of securing funds for the ministry of the local church and the district association. It would be wise to understand the "Yesterday reasoning" that leaders taught their members. Among pastors, the old wisdom about giving was, "We don't have to persuade people to support the ministry; that's God job." The new wisdom is, " We must effetely convey to our people what we stand for, how we minister and what difference it makes in people's lives. The new wisdom is not a repudiation of the old prospective, but a recognition that times have changed, and we must do a greater share of the work to prepare people to sense God's direction in our lives. Simply waiting for God to touch peoples heart with a desire to give money to the cause may sound more spiritual, but the new wisdom is certainly a reflection of practical theology, based on James 4:2-3:kjv "You do not have because you do not ask God. When you ask you do not receive, because you as with the wrong motives, that you may spend what you get on your pleasures"

There is a strange phenomenon that goes on in the mine of the brothers and sisters who comes out of the local church to take on this great task. They must cease to think about themselves, for now is the time to keep the organization and it administrative purpose in focus. They must now be vigilant, watchful of God working within His creation, and sober in his daily life-style, so that they are listening whenever God speak.. Listening to God has never been easy, and many times we are not sure when he is speaking But there is one way to be in His will for our lives, but the traveling man who occupies this road will run into obstacles after and on top of each other. What is that one way? Faith in Jesus Christ and believing in his word.

There are three ways a Christian can give and supply sufficient funds for his local church, District Association, and on the state level. These people who have been chosen for the journey, must realize that the church is one intuition that does not provide revenue within itself. The D.A. spends money that comes from the pocket of church membership. They must have the mindset and attitude to work with the pastors to achieve the financial need of the local church and the D.A..

Here again, and don't forget this statement. People no longer give to the church or the D.A. because it is what it is. They must prove it is worthy of the donations through the mark it leaves on the world. On the other hand donors or givers look for organizations of which they have a heart connection--A shared cause that make the organization a compelling recipient of funds. Donors, givers don't give to intuition. They invest in ideas and people to whom they believe.

He must believe and teach others to believe that neither he nor anyone else can out give God and that God stand ready to share His blessings and promises with us at a level that we have never seen before.Rev. King you and your people must remember that change requires action. Most people wait until they feel like it to change their attitude. But that only causes them to keep waiting because they have the whole process backward. If you wait until you feel like it to try to change your attitude. You will never change. "You have to act yourself into changing." Part of that change is having a positive idea of what the meaning of success.

Some people think that success is due to a man being brilliant in knowledge. Some. Some think that it is magic--something which we do not possess. What then is success? Most people have a vague picture of what it means to be a successful person. Probably the most common misunderstanding about success is that it's the same as having money. King Solomon stated, "Whoever loves money never has enough; whoever loves wealth is never satisfied with his income." Wealth and what it brings are at least fleeting. Let us look at a definition of success; (Knowing your purpose in life, growing to reach your maximum potential, and sowing seed that benefit others.) The people taking this journey will never exhaust his capacity to grow toward his potential or run out of opportunities to help others.

(The tithe and offering) that the membership shares with the Lord under the leadership of the pastor and deacons goes to the local church, the sacrificial gift that, that same member gives goes to the building fund.

It is a small amount after the tithe and offering. The Tithe began at 10% FROM THE TOP OF WHAT God has provided him as income. The tithe should go up not down, unless something happens that you cannot pay. Then go back to God and ask him if you can pay a less amount, until he blesses you. Whatever the amount that you promise, make sure that you give that. Never forget that He comes first./ Your gift to the ministries of the church such as Sunday school, brotherhood, mission and dues, should be paid if you promised to pay them.

(Sacrificial Gift) It does not matter how poor one may be, he can give a quarter each Sunday, or go up as high as a hundred dollars on a regular basis. The sacrificial gift is all that he/she has to give; it is an amount that is present but is for another use. But they are going to sacrifice for the sake of the need of God's house. It can and should be small enough that the giver will continue to give over a long period of time. It is a sacrifice, and a sacrifice hurts from time to time. There are times that you can barely see your way. But with the help of God you are able to make the journey.

There is a (third part of this concept.) The money that we want to give is not presently available to us. In other words we do not have the money that we want to give. We formulate the amount that we want to give, and then we will go to God with our request and our desire to give what we do not have. We will believe that God is going to provide the funds for us to give to the project, but if he does not, we cannot give what we desire Example; I desire to give the church or project $5,000,00 at the end of the year. AFTER I GIVE MY TITHE AND OFFERING, I DO NOT HAVE IT TO GIVE. If God will provide the resources I will give it, if he does not, I do not have it to give. Whether I give it or nor is depending upon God. The only qualification that I am responsible for, is that I walk with Him in his Holiness and obedience. The three ways of giving should be the foundational basis for the leadership of this project. The leadership and follower ship role in furthering the church on its way to God's will. The three ways of giving do put anymore financial responsibility upon the believer, but it changes his attitude and open up avenues for God to bless the church and its membership.

Rev. Kings attention was drawn to a noise that he heard and saw what was not there, but yet there it stood in testimony of the task that lie ahead of him. He looked toward the door in the left hand corner of the room and there he saw what was there, but it had no way of telling a human who they were. The (forward spirit) told him that it was the wind. It was almost like a ball or one of the planets in the solar system. It was streaky round in a light blue color, mixed with a shade of tight red, with just a taste of brown and yellow. He knew that he could not see air, but then in the second and third heaven, around the throne where the trinity resides, humans know not what the atmosphere produces. The wind in front of him, no larger than 22 balls of matter; and it had a message. A message for a man in the second heaven. He wanted to ask God for an understanding, but God was busy in the message that the wind was delivering. Not so busy that He could not answer, but saw no need to respond to a human interference.)

In the preceding message he was asked a question. How well do you know what God wants you to do? Are you so sure that you know, that you would give your life for the mystery that lie ahead of you. Think for a moment, you are a preacher and a pastor, but do you know what God want you to do? Sure you know that you are a preacher, to share the good news on Sunday morning, but where do you go from there? You must know what every person you chose, and you must be able to teach them the root meaning of all their gifts. All of the people that you choose must know or learn what God want them to do, before the journey began. There is no place for error, mistake, or unforgiving sin, they must be confident of their calling and spiritual gift. They must be so confident of their calling, that no hesitation is required before they act. Do not let the buzzard land in your tree, but carry the raven wherever you go. The rabbit will take care of himself and protect you on narrow, rocky, dusty roads that leads to the cross.

Rev. King found his first instructions, a word of wisdom and knowledge to be strange coming from Him. It is unfair to the church and your organization to allow a believer to operate as a leader without the knowledge of his or her gifts. THEY ARE THE ONE'S THAT WILL HELP TO PREPARE God's people for work of service, so that the body of Christ may be built up. Build up until we all reach unity in the faith and in knowledge of the son of God and become mature.

Attaining to the whole measure of the fullness of Christ (Eph. 4:12-13) Ask your self it said with a bitten voice of concern. Can you be saved if you do not have a spiritual gifts? Then he followed with; are there consequences if a believer does not operate within his spiritual gift area.?

The folding words from the wind--there was a silence, something here was out of place. Wind and words, he thought about when God spoke things into existence. They came forward as if they had already been there, full grown. No Christian can please God without the believer knowing their spiritual gift. Nothing can make a Christian life more exciting and fulfilling than the discovery of ones spiritual gift or gifts. Without the operational results of ones spiritual gift, a Christian's life will be dull, spiritless, lifeless, lack luster and uninspired. And why shouldn't it be, for that person has decided not to obey God in their spiritual gift.

CHAPTER #6

The reason for spiritual gifts

Where there is no counsel, the people fall, but in the multitude of counselors there is safety. (Prov. 11:14)

Why do you think God give us a spiritual gift? Is it because it allows for a powerful relationship? This relationship joins believer with their father so they can be heirs and joint heirs with Jesus Christ. It put them into a position so that His promises and blessings stand ready to deliver their positive results. More than any other single thing, discovering our spiritual gift help us find God's will for our lives. To know our spiritual gift is to have concrete and specific direction in life. Finding our spiritual gifts is like a road sign to a lost and weary traveler.. It shows us the direction we should take to reach our destination in the Christian life.

Many believers are looking for excitement and purpose in life and shouldn't they? This Christian life has purpose and it is exciting. One must experience and discover your spiritual gift's to be set free from bondage of not knowing what God's will is for your life. Most believers who are discourage and find the Christian life dull are those who have not found, or are not using their spiritual gifts. When you choose these people, make sure that when you choose them, there is a place for their gift's. A place that will move the project of the D.A. forward. This will not be as easy as it now seem. To endure through the tough times that lie ahead will cause a dedication just a little out of reach than where we usually travel. Sometime you will have to read Luke 22:39- To gain some comfort.

Discovering one's spiritual gifts will make the Christian life more vivacious and more meaningful than anything that one have experience.

But be careful, because it takes time, effort, and discipline to find one's spiritual gifts. This is said with tongue in cheek. The reason is that the giver of the gift is the same one who wants the believer to put the gifts into operation. He never ceases to be concerned when the task of spiritual gifts become to difficult to handle. The place to investigate them is the Bible. We must study them in their proper Biblical context. We cannot rely on hearsay or the experience of others. We must come to understand them based on sound Biblical facts. Nothing can enlighten one more than concerning spiritual gifts than investigating them in the Bible.

Not only should we investigate the discovery of our gift through the Bible and listen to the truth of the Holy Spirit. The first step is to investigate. The second step is to participate in the study of the Bible. Until we have shown our love and respect for the Bible by obeying its commands, it will not be helpful in discovering our spiritual gifts.. But we must learn to participate, to operate in the gift. Yes it will open us up to spiritual things that we have never experience before. But the spirit belongs to God; his son Jesus Christ sent him to us. We need not fear anything that the spirit does. It has come as our comforter.

Because God knows us so well, he perfectly matches our personalities and abilities to our spiritual gifts, so that when used they bring immense joy. This is probably the most surprising part of discovering our spiritual gifts or gift. You must be aware that many Christians never really try to find their spiritual gift because they think God is a "KILLJOY." They have never realized gifts bring joy and satisfaction because the deepest wishes and desires of our heart will be fulfilled. To discover our spiritual gifts, we must investigate, participate, evaluate, and finally cultivate. Once the spiritual gift is discovered, it must be cultivated. Gifts are like seeds that grow and produce fruit when properly cultivated through use.

As you cultivate your gift, remember it is to make you and your organization more like Christ. In 1 Corinthian 12:1. Paul says, "Now concerning spiritual gifts, brethren, I do not want you to be ignorant." Then in the following verse, he compares the gifts of the spirit to eyes, ears hands, and feet in the body of Christ. Using the same illustration of a body, what purpose does Paul give for spiritual gifts in Ephesians 4:16.? In explaining spiritual gifts, the question often arises, "What is the difference between spiritual gifts and talents.

Talents are also given by God but are usually derived genetically from parents. The difference between a talent and a gift is probably best illustrated by the fact Billy Graham ask of George Beverly Shea sings just before he preaches. When ask why, Dr. Graham explain that George Shea never performs; he always ministers. A talent performs: A gift, ministers. Spiritual gifts make us minister not perform.

Many times Christians look at Spiritual Gifts as a whole, but it is best to know them individually. As a whole you use the combination of gifts. But individually, you study the knowledge of each gift. Every Christian man who has opened the door of heaven here on earth, has at least one spiritual gift. Most Christians have more than one, and yet most Christians are afraid of what God want them to do. Look at these gifts individually, study them, know what the definition for each one spells out. Look then at 1 Corinthians 12:1-11.,

TAKE YOUR TIME AND DON'T BE AFRAID TO LEARN WHAT God has in store for you. If you cannot learn or will not learn, then the men and women who walks with you may never accomplish this task. No man should walk on this earth, step inside a sanctuary or bow down on his knees, without knowing that the blood that Jesus shared was not a waste. Every man and woman that you choose, must know their spiritual gift or gifts. They must be so embedded into their souls, that every day the gifts show themselves.

The gifts is to stress the essential unity of the church. The church is the body of Christ and the characteristic of an healthy body is that every part in it performs its own function for the good of the whole; but unity does not mean uniformity, and there forth with the church there are different gifts and different functions. But everyone of them is a gift of the same spirit and designed, not for the glory of the individual member of the church, but for the good of the whole. No scripture drives home the purpose of the Gifts that God gives to his family members like Eph.4:11-13 He shares in this scripture what he has given to the church through its leadership. There are some who call these, the five fold ministries of the church. But to you they are instruction to you and those you choose. You must understand them, you would do well to remember this scripture from memory. Revised Standard: 4:11-13 (Eph.) "And his gifts were that some should be apostles, some prophets, some evangelists, some pastors and teachers.-to equip the saints for the work of the ministry for building up the body of Christ, until we all attain to the unity of the faith and of the knowledge of the Son of God, to mature manhood, to the measure of stature of the fullness of Christ."

In Luke 4:18 He shares with the people of the living God, and give them a bird eye view of what the church is about. He shares with his own what to look out for as to the deepness of his word, the intentions of where he is leading them, and to the leaders of the church a command. Listen carefully, and as you listen agree with your soul you will obey.

"The spirit of the Lord is upon me,
Because he has anointed me to preach good
News to the poor.
He has sent me to proclaim release to the
Captives,
And recovering of sight to the blind,
To set at liberty those who are oppressed"

Here my brother lays the instructions for the church and to you a road map for the pastors of the district association.. Each of them must make sure that they do not rob the church in not carrying out these instructions. For with them they carry a heavy responsibility that pastors and leaders cannot ignore.

WISDOM/KNOWLEDGE.

Spiritual gifts are for both the pastors, leaders and saints of the local church. For this purpose let us began with 1 Corinthians 12:1-11, for the purpose intended the whole scripture will not be read. Here are the gifts for those that you recruit. Wisdom and knowledge, they sound alike but does not mean the same thing. Wisdom. "The knowledge of things human and divine and of their causes. Wisdom; is the wisdom which knows God. Knowledge is more practical for every day life. It is the knowledge which knows what in any given situation. It is the practical application to hums life and affairs. Two things are necessary -the wisdom which knows by communion with God the deep things of God, and knowledge which, in the daily life of the world and the church, can put wisdom into practice.

FAITH: Here faith means more than ordinary faith. It is the faith which really produces results. It is not just the intellectual conviction that a thing is true; it is the passionate belief in a thing which makes a man spend all that he is and has on it. It is the faith that steels the will and nerves the sinew of a man in action. This kind of faith turns a mans vision into deeds. This kind of faith when shared from the bottom of a man's soul, will cause mountains in our lives to run toward the sea and rivers turn and go upstream.

SPECIAL GIFTS OF HEALING: There is not the slightest doubt that gifts of healing did exist in the early church; It is no doubt that through faith in Jesus Christ, healing can and has been a source of the power of the church. In the letter of James (5:14) there is an instruction that if a man is ill he must come to the elders and they will anoint him with oil. The church never altogether lost this gift of healing; and in recent times it has been somewhat rediscovered. For too long the Church split man into a soul and a body, and accepted responsibility for his soul but not for his body It is good that in our time we have once again learn to treat man as a whole. WONDERFUL DEEDS OF POWER. Almost certainly this refers to exorcisms. In the days past illnesses, often all illnesses, and especially mental illnesses, were attributed to the work of demons; and it was one of the functions to exorcise these demons. Today demons approaches believers in a different manner, they will take whatever space the believer allows them to have and build up doubt in their minds to the point that Satan controls that part of a believers life. The brother or sister who attempts to relieve the soul from the demons, must be perfect at the time he attempts to cast the demon out. What this all mean is; the servant must be under total control of the Holy Spirit. The spirit must speak to him, giving him the o.k. to relieve the believer from the bonds of Satan. If the servant has any un-repented sin, it will stand between him and God. Satan will recognize as being himself and his angels. There can not be any deliverance until the perfect will of God is represented and take control. The deliverer must look beyond the eye balls of the believer, into the depth of his soul and speak in the name of Jesus, under the blood that was shared shed on Calvery cross. In the name of Jesus Christ the son of the living God, I demand that you loosen him and come out of him, in Jesus name. If you do not have the unction from God to do the deliverance, I would let it alone. I would lay hands on him and pray for his deliverance to be soon.

PROPHECT:

There are many who give this word as preaching, but for your cause it is the man who lives so close to God that he knows his mind and heart and will, and so can make them known to men. Because of that his function is twofold. (A) He brings rebuke and warning, telling men that their way of action is not in accordance with the will of God. (B) He brings advice and guidance, seeking to direct men into the ways God wishes them to go.

Before you start doing a deliverance, remember that you are in a Spiritual Warfare, that demon powers are set in array in a chain of command. Satan has his representatives assigned over nations, cities, churches, homes and individual lives. The scripture instruct us to engage this power structure in spiritual warfare, therefore, take authority over all higher powers that have authority over the demons indwelling the one being set free. Bind off these higher powers from interfering in any way with the ministry. Then bind the "strong man" OR RULING SPIRIT WHICH IS OVER THE LESSER DEMONS THAT indwell the person." Or else how can one enter into a strongman's house and spoil his goods, except he first bind the strong man? And then he will spoil the house. Matt.12:29

DISTINGUISH BETWEEN DIFFERENT KINDS OF SPIRITS.

In a society where the atmosphere was tense and where all kinds of manifestations were normal, it was necessary to distinguish between what was real and what merely hysterical, between what came from God and what came from the devil. To this day, when a thing is outside our ordinary orbit, it is supremely difficult to tell whether it is from God or not. The one principal to observe is that we must always try to understand before we condemn. The spirit of God who is in control will make it clear that he is speaking. If we allow Satan to help us make decisions, we may find ourselves in a hole of trouble. Quick decisions and at the moment decisions may cause us to make spiritual mistakes. Always take the time to hear from God, he is listening.

THE GIFTS OF TONGUES/THE ABILITY TO INTERPRET THEM.

This matter of tongues caused a great deal of perplexity in the Corinth church. And being a pastor you know that there are difficulties concerning tongues today. The cause is simple, but the solution is not simple.

What happen was this-- a church service someone would fall into an ecstasy and pout out a torrent of unintelligible sounds in no known language. This was a highly covered gift because it was suppose to be due to the direct influence of the Spirit of God. To the congregation it was of course completely meaningless. Sometime the person so moved could interpret his own outpouring, but usually it required someone who had the gift of interpretation. Never question the reality of the gifts of tongues. Paul was well aware that it had its dangers, for ecstasy and a kind of self-hypnotism are very difficult to distinguish. Today's church is not alive as the church in days past. Astonishing things happen, that does not happen in todays church. Life was heightened and intensified. There were nothing dull and ordinary about the early church. The prophets knew that all this vivid, powerful activity was the work of the Spirit who gave to each man his gift to use for all.

A table appeared in the middle of the floor. The table were black and white squares, with little roving red eyes that looked as if they was coming out of a panhandle dust storm. In each of the chairs around the table a set of red eyes took their position. There were not a chair for the moderator, but he was comfortable standing near the moving table. He could clearly hear every thing that was said, but he could not understand what was being told to him.

He was comfortable in the world where he was. But where was he, it was not earth and its surroundings. It was not heaven; he could not see the father or the Son. Yet it was a place that he had never been. It was a place where sin did not have any reason to exist. Matter of fact no sin, no thought of disobedience or thought of doing wrong resided in this place of time. He was allowed to know that he was there for a purpose, but whatever the purpose was, was placed in his inner mind, when needed it will rise to the occasion. He felt as if he was being elevated. He felt as if he was sitting in an invisible chair, caught in a small whirlwind that quietly lifted him up slowly from its bottom. He felt as if he was whirling to the point of not recognizing anything. Finally he saw a heavenly choir that looked like skinny cedar trees, they were singing but he never heard a word. The tree people grew until he recognized that he was in the presence of God. That he was not here on earth and that he was not yet in heaven. He was spaced in time for a visit that he may or may not remember.

But a time that will affect his life as long as he lives on this earth. His feeling without knowing where he was screamed softly that they were in the second heaven. A place where only God the father, his Son and the Holy Spirit would occasional visit some Saints from His creation.

The moderator did not have control of himself, neither was there any thought about God's creation.(Or thought about anything that God had created.) he was spaced in time and nothing about the earth settled on his God given mind. Strange thing, though he knew that he was in some part of heaven; he did not see the Father or the Son. But some one spoke in a soft, but stern voice. It was a language that he knew nothing about. And all this time he just recognized that someone had his hand on his shoulder. A person he never saw. Assuring him that all was going to be all right, that the Father would take care of His own. In this environment one could not last more than a minute or two, and even then he needed heavenly assistance to return to earth. The words filled the room, it was not like talking; It filled the room with its presence. There could be no doubts that it was God speaking. The father was speaking to the moderator in His son's native language, Arabic.

يا بني، يكون قويا وشجاعا جدا. كن حريصا على طاعة كل شريعتي "
أعطى موسى عبده كنت لا يرجع عنه إلى اليمين أو إلى اليسار، والتي قد تكون ناجحة في
أي مكان تذهب إليه. لا تدع هذا الكتاب من القانون تغادر من فمك. التأمل في ذلك ليلا
ونهارا، لذلك والتي قد تكون حريصا على ألا يفعل كل ما هو مكتوب فيه.
فإنك سوف تكون مزدهرة وناجحة. أنا لم أمركم؟ كن قويا وشجاعا. لا يكون بالرعب. لا تثبط،
لأن الرب إلهك يكون معك أينما ذهبت. الاستماع عن كثب ابني هذه الكلمات يجب أن يذهب
معك أينما ذهبت.

نهاية كل شيء قد اقتربت. لذلك يكون واضحا الذهن والنفس التي تسيطر عليها بحيث
يمكنك صلاة. قبل كل شيء، نحب بعضنا البعض كثيرا، لأن المحبة تستر كثرة من الخطايا.
تقديم الضيافة لبعضها البعض دون تذمر. يجب أن تستخدم كل واحد أيا كان هدية تلقاها
لخدمة الآخرين. إدارة بأمانة نعمة الله في أشكاله المختلفة. إذا يتحدث أي شخص، يجب أن
يفعل ذلك واحدا يتكلم بلسان الله نفسها. إذا يخدم أحدا، فعليه أن يفعل ذلك مع قوة يوفر الله،
بحيث في كل شيء قد يكون مدح الله من خلال يسوع المسيح
أيها الأصدقاء، لا يكون مفاجأة في التجارب المؤلمة كنت تعاني، كما لو كانت شيئا غريبا \
يحدث لك. إلا أن نبتهج أن تشارك في معاناة المسيح، بحيث قد تكون بسعادة غامرة عندما
يتم كشف مجده. إذا أهان لك بسبب اسم المسيح \ ل، وأنعم عليك، لأن روح المجد والله باقي
عليك. لذلك حان الوقت للحكم على بدأ مع عائلة الله واذا بدأ معنا، ماذا ستكون النتيجة
بالنسبة لأولئك الذين لا يطيعون إنجيل الله. "من الصعب للمتقين ليتم حفظها، ما سيكون
مصير الفجار وخاطيء" حتى ذلك الحين، وأولئك الذين يعانون وفقا لإرادة الله يجب أن
"تلتزم خالقهم المؤمنين والاستمرار في فعل الخير.

"My son, be strong and very courageous. Be careful to obey all the law my servant Moses gave you do not turn from it to the right or to the left, that you may be successful wherever you go. Do not let this book of the law depart from your mouth; meditate on it day and night, so that you may be careful to do everything written in it. Then you will be prosperous and successful. Have I not commanded you? Be strong and courageous. Do not be terrified; do not be discouraged, for the Lord your God will be with you wherever you go. Listen closely my son these words must go with you wherever you go.

The end of all things is near. Therefore be clear minded and self-controlled so that you can pray. Above all, love each other dearly, because love covers a multitude of sins. Offer hospitality to one another without grumbling. Each one should use whatever gift he has received to serve others. Faithfully administering God's grace in its various forms. If anyone speaks, he should do it as one speaking the very words of God. If anyone serves,, he should do it with the strength God provides, so that in all things God may be praised through Jesus Christ.

Dear Friends, do not be surprise at the painful trials you are suffering, as though something strange were happening to you. But rejoice that you participate in the suffering of Christ., so that you may be overjoyed when His glory is revealed. If you are insulted because of the name of Christ\For, you are blessed, for the Spirit of glory and of God rest on you. For it is time for judgment to began with the family of God and if it began with us, what will the outcome be for those who does not obey the gospel of God. "It is hard for the righteous to be saved, what will become of the ungodly and the sinner" So then, those who suffer according to God's will should commit themselves to their faithful Creator and continue to do good.

The moderator knew it was God speaking to him, but what was he to do, He had no control over anything. He did not see God at any time, he did not see the son, nor did he observe the nature of the Holy Spirit. He would have been confused if he was here on earth, but that thought never crossed his mind. The only thing that he saw was the shadow of a cross dripping in blood that did not have a resting place to call its own. There were a small, distant noise, that came from the wind around the Jordan river that had settled somewhere near the cross. The shadow of the cross, showed it to be different than any cross that God's creation had ever seen. It was strange, why they even called it a cross.

The room where he was were lighted so brightly until he had to put his hands over his face with his eyes closed. The place where he had met Jesus was so bright until all candles and light and light bulbs, whether they were in the socket of not, lighted up.

Rev. King coming out of the second heaven found his room so lighted until he had to cover his eyes, and even then the light blinded him. The walls around the room began to disappear into nothingness. It was replaced with a wall of Gold and other minerals that he knew nothing of. The beauty of the new wall, could not be described in human language. This was a wonder to behold. He reached out and he could feel the brightness between his fingers. It was soft, and it barely had a structure enough for him to feel. His body seemed to be surrounded by a foggy mist that he could not see. The light of the gold walls gave a string sound as if someone was playing a string instrument.

For the first few minutes of the conference they only spoke Arabic, then the eyes choose a body and a head, but no one was recognizable. The wind was still present and it was he who spoke. It was the hand that rested itself on his shoulder. "Your inner mind will carry a message that you will not remember. But it will never leave you, don't pay any attention to what you hear. The only person that you will have to listen each day is your father. I will place people in your way and you can't help but see them. When you know who they are, they will be the group that I want you to have. If you don't understand all that is going on and at the speed that they are happening, don't let it concern you. There is a space of emptiness between here and there. I will fill that space and the results of this conversation will bring success to your door step.

Every organization that has been put together for my benefit, has moved into a state of demise. They do not respect me, they have no faith in the words that I speak, They don't trust me and they have forgotten who I am and what I have gone through for my creation. Look at them on Sunday morning, they are going through the motions, their prayers have failed to tough any compassion for help. This may be the last chance in this area for repentance, last chance for forgiveness, and it may be the last chance for some of them to face me for mercy, grace has grown tired of them stacking sin on top of sin without even asking forgiveness. Un-forgiveness and un-repentance has only a short time to fall at the feet of Jesus, and get back on that narrow road to eternal life.

When he came to himself, the pipe was in the trash can, and all his tobacco had been burned. He sat there in his chair wondering where he had been. He did not know, but he knew that he had been somewhere, that he wished that he would never leave again.

But he did not understand the confusion that racked his mind and how it shifted to peace in the house. His cabinet was wide open and not a bottle of anything remained in the cabinet. He knew that he was prepared for something, but the D.A. had not crossed his mind. Sitting there he thought about the journey ahead of him, but by now he could not think about the conference he just had. He can't even remembering leaving the room. He just felt as if something had happen. His mind, his heart, his eyes and his soul held a secret that will be revealed to him in time. Even then he will not know where he came across the enlightenment that rocked his soul.

Things of this world began to come back to him. He remembered the evening that the breaking up of the D.A. Begun. It started innocent enough, and when it ended no one said a word, they just kept quiet. It was in this meeting that the moderator made a terrible mistake, and the D.A. backed him up. The moderator was a powerful preacher and he held many I.O.U. notes in his pocked. But before he would pull one out, he would look at the preacher to let him know that he would pull the note and call in his I.O.U. Some of the preachers would fall into a cold sweat and began trembling. He held power and he used it when he had to put some preacher in their place. He had made a statement that caused a chuckle at the time. He asked for the roll call of the D.A., those who had not paid what they had promised was discharged from the association. No effort was made to contact the pastors or the churches, they were dismissed from the district Association without being contacted. From that time until now that organization began to crumble and fall apart. When the district called its meeting after this incident, people just did not come. Many of the Churches who had supported this organization threw their Hands up in disgust. Only a few in this large metropolitan area stayed true and tried to help keep it together.

The wind looked across the table from where the pastor who was standing, stood. What do you first suggest. He raise himself, batted his eyes a few times: Go back 15 years, take the book that kept all the names of pastors and churches. Put all of the churches who are in good standing, with their pastor, name of the church, address and city. List if they have an active brotherhood. Share with the rest of us how much they give a year, or whenever they were suppose to give.

Total it up and see how much all incoming income is total. Figure out from the years of expense and the books that goes 15 years back. What are the expense of the D.A., leave nothing out, all expenses must be included. What is the difference between the income and the expense. Then he sat down.

The person who sat next to him was fidgeting with his pencil that had an eraser on both ends. He stood, there were no indication of where he was looking, then he spoke; As you can see there is a wide difference between the income and the expenses. Second the money that we call expense goes to preachers, very few persons who is a layman receive pay for anything in the D.A.. Third, what do the layman who attends the sessions take back home with him, and how can he use what he has learned at his local church. Churches who give to the association, do not get their money's worth of learning and understanding. They have nothing or a very little to take to the home church that will benefit the church.. The local church and the association is not on the same page. Matter of fact there is little interest in the local church, outside of their walls. The local church has forgotten to keep its membership vivid and alive. Many have little pride in their church or their pastor, some almost hang their head when their church is mentioned. The church must be taught the word and give each member an opportunity to respond to the will of God.

Many of today's pastors, their motive and their attitudes are a disgrace to the gospel of Jesus Christ. Many who mount the pulpit are not saved, neither have they been called to share the gospel. Yet, they pastor churches and mislead the congregation. Some teach that homosexual is just another sin, some have been taught by older preachers to get all the money you can. Others says find a woman that you admire and have sex with her until you get her under your control. There are some who will chose a man for a bed partner, as long as he has money and will spend it. There are some who desire power, power and more power. They will take the gospel, turn it around to fit what they want to accomplish. None of these kind of people will be allowed in this group. If people get angry with you and call you perfect, complete, a saint. Remind them that all three terms that they use are those who are obedient to the word of God.

In the Eastern part of the room sat two eyes that all the rest was uncomfortable with. He was the only one of the four that did not set still. His eyes did not go from side to side, they went from up to down, not fast but slowly and his body seem to be trembling even though he did not move anything but his eyes. Then he spoke almost as if he was afraid. Finally, if you are going to teach eternal salvation, make sure that they get the best understanding of the word and its concept.

Remember this scripture, if not from memory, remember what it mean. (Heb. 6:4. living Bible) "There is no use trying to bring you back to the lord again if you have once understood the good news and tasted for yourself the good things of heaven and shared in the Holy Spirit, and know how good the word of God is, and felt the mighty powers of the world to come, and then have turned against God. You cannot bring yourself to repent again if you have nailed the Son of God to the cross again by rejecting him, holding him up to mocking and public shame."

If you come in contact with a pastor who is having an affair with a female/male in his church; if he feels as if he is not going to stop his activity, after you have talked with him in private, make your report immediately to Rev. King. From then on you will not have anything to do with this case. You will write the case from your files, give it a heading and number, then file it away. If you happen to contact a pastor who teaches hell and heaven, but does not believe there is life after death, take his file to Rev. King for further investigation. If a pastor believes that church membership should do what he tells them to do. He believes that he will hear from God in his own way, and then he will interrupt God's words to suit his comfort zone. Be careful with him. Take his file to headquarters and see if he can be convinced to obey God's word. If a pastor is a person who abuse women, including his wife, see if you can get him some physiology help, if not remove him from the list. It is also with gambling, this is a disease and it destroy many families and they don't know what hit them. When you talk to the pastor and his wife or the chairman of the board, observe them carefully, watch their body language it says volume's about who and what they are.

What goes for the pastor also goes for the deacons. Takes notes and keep them.

The eyes now looked steady at the wind that was against the wall, and for a moment there was silence throughout the room. Then the eyes was focused on the subject at hand. The eyes spoke, you will have to have a compassion for each church, its pastor, the chairman of the deacon board (and the church). It is not your responsibility to tell them, but to share with them what you believe is the directions that come from God. They must understand there is a need for them with the D.A. that needs to be fulfilled. No one can fill that need except that church group. Do not beg them, but help them to see how men and women working together can be a benefit for all concerned.

Whenever you feel as if they think that you are a big cheese, back off, by all means stay humble, and always how this coming together will benefit all.

Have a copy of the book, The Brother Up Next, instruct them that the D.A. Will be structure around the Bible, but the book of study will be The Brother Up Next, the administration and doctrine of the Church, and above all The Holy Bible. Make sure a copy of all three written material is available and handed to each pastor. The group will make sure that these books are available. They will be purchased at half priced book store or used on Amazon.com There cannot be any excuse, not even a tiny reason to fail. Give them a copy of the book and set up another appointment for their discussion. Between the meeting and the upcoming gathering call the pastor, talk about light things that is going on in the world. Make it brief, unless he wants to extend the conversation. You are at his beck and call. But try to find out what he expects of the D.A. and what he can give in spiritual resources. Make him feel important, but never put him too high that if he comes in he will be disappointed. He has to see that as a group what could be accomplished. Ask him if he had time to look at the book that you had left with him.

The same process will be used with each church that has strayed away. Remember there has to be some change made. But be careful with change, people normally do not like change. Make change slowly, and clarify the meaning of what you are trying to get over. And yet, some of the moves that is to be made is different and maybe hard for some to swallow. No one wants to come back to the same old thing. Remember that if they come back, they will be looking for that change to be evident. Hopefully all the churches that returns will have Christian brothers as pastors. And they are willing to give themselves to the Lord for his directions. (Luke 14:26-30, 33KJV) "If any man come to me, and hate not his father, and mother, and wife, and children, and brethren, and sisters, yea, and his own life also, he cannot be my disciple. And whosoever doth not bear his cross, and come after me, cannot be my disciple. For which of you, intending to build a tower sitteth not down first and count the cost.

Nothing concerning the house of faith, should be done without first counting the cost. Some time the cost is too deep, the sacrifice too steep. We don't want to promise God that we will do a thing, and then find out the cost is too much. A dropped head is just the tip of the ice berg, a disappointed soul can find no way of escape.

He must live a life through circumstances that he has never experienced before. A heavy heart can sometime become to heavy for the chest to contain. When that happens, breathing becomes difficult, and you look for air that is so plentiful, air that you can feel and yet realize that it may not keep the heart ticking, you are not sure if this is your time, but if it wasn't for the consequence of dying, you would take your last breath and go home.

The air now looks like a fall sunrise, different colors takes it's place in the air's presence form. The words that he spoke was a little un expected and King could feel his hand on his shoulder. A hand of structure and support. Then he spoke, I don't know which way that you are leaning, but I must make myself clear. We cannot allow the least suspicious of slackness at the top of the upper level. If God's word is not clear of any action that we may become involved with, we will not do it. If we are wrong, we will be wrong on the side of strictness. Being slack will never be a part of our teaching, preaching or our worship service. We need the best that God has to offer, and we need his help so that we can share with him the best that we have. Therefore When you find a pastor who allows a woman into his pulpit to bring a message, inform him of his wrongness, if you get an argument from him, turn his folder in for further investigation. But you will not touch that pastor or church. It could be that they do not know any better, then on the other hand, that may be their belief. If one of the persons that you are checking out informs you that she is a preacher, she believe that she have been called to preach the gospel. Do not argue with her, do not try to show her how she is wrong. Especially about mounting the pulpit. Let someone with a special revelation from the Lord share what the Good Lord has to say. This is especially true if she is a member of the local church. Many churches who have broken off from the D.A. is now allowing women to preach and stand in the pulpit. Now that you have heard the instructions of the father pertaining to these things. It is now time to formulate a program that will help you to be successful.

The door to the room opened and it was daylight outside. The buzzard walked out first, looked at a dead tree limb and without temptation to rise up and land he walked into nothingness. The Ravine appeared to be happy and almost jolly of laughter if it was possible. Then he walked away. The rabbit sat at the side of the door watching the other two disappear into the sunshine. He dropped his head as thou he was in deep thought, he looked around in the room then he hopped away with all four legs. No one made a sound, not even a cough. Every thing in the house disappeared, the eyes, the pencil, the animals and the wind, their responsibility had come to an end, but they would always be on alert, watching and waiting for the masters call.

Rev. King stretched his legs, by walking to the close door. When he opened it he found morning had set in over the trees. He stood in the door for a while, something just wasn't quite right, he did not feel comfortable. For one thing he did not know where his wife was. He could remember seeing her move around in the back of him in the room. But she looked as if she was in a foggy mist, and at no time did she look directly At him. It was as if she did not want him to take on the responsibility that lie ahead of him. Surely taking on this great task, would take much time from her and what she wanted him to do. Each time that he saw her even in a daze, she was not happy. When he walked out the door, he realized that he was in a small country town---but he lived in the Dallas/Ft. Worth area

He looked for his pipe, but it was on the table, he needed something to calm his nerves. But he had no desire to smoke the pipe, as much as he loved the pipe, today he did not want it. He reached inside his coat pocket and pulled out a camel cigarette, When he reached for a light, he remembered that he had promised himself that he would stop smoking, and he made sure that he left all things to light a smoke, would not be in his pocket.. He looked at the cigarette, remembered the promise that he made. He took the cigarette, buried it under some sand on the ground. When he raised up he saw the cemetery that is in throwing distant of the house. The strange thing was he had never see the cemetery before. He looked, and then he looked and then he looked again, but the cemetery would not go away. The first grave he could see from just our side the door, but when he got closer, there were another fresh grave occupied by a woman who happen to be a saint. The grave seem to be pulling him toward where the bodies lay, when he got close he saw a little one foot tall stool and he knew it was for his benefit. When he sat on the stool he could almost feel something trembling, as if someone was getting up. The wind stilled itself and a darkness came over them.

Then he remembered the scripture from the 28th chapter of 1

Samuel, A scripture that caused him to trembled, because he could not understand why this scripture had come to mind. Not only did it come to mind, but it burst through the grave and sat beside him on the stool. It was as real as a man sitting beside him for conversation. He never saw a person, but he felt the presence of a (unfamiliar spirit.)

And then there was an image of an old man wrapped in a white robe, with a red piece of cloth tied around his waste. The old man never looked up, but he held his hands toward him as if he was offering him up in prayer. King wanted to be in another place, but the power to move did not belong to him. He was comfortable, but he could not move. He wanted to be out of this atmosphere and into another environment. He felt a little confused, but he was never out of control; there was always a hand holding him steady.

On the ground beside the grave where the fresh dirt had found a resting place of the living dead. He saw words that he remembered, but now knowing that they have to mean something else than before. They were not exactly, word for word as he knew it to be in the Bible. They were to open up a meaning in his head, but before it did he was reminded that he was in the second heaven. His flesh did not respond as in the natural sense, for here it had no control over anything. But his mind did not understand all that was going on, yet his spirit did not miss a word. When the outcome of the vision needed for him to know, all things will be in place. For now he heard the words and saw onto a field of time what was happening long before Christ came on the scene. He saw before him scenes being acted out as if he was standing in Ramah, where Samuel was buried.

"When Saul saw the vast army of the philistine, he was frantic with fear and asked the Lord what he should do. But the Lord refused to answer him., either by dreams, or by urim, or by the prophets. Saul then instructed his aids to try to find a medium so that he could ask her what to do, and they found one at Endor. Saul disguised himself by wearing ordinary clothes instead of his royal robe. He went to the woman's home at night, accompanied by two of his men.

'I've got to talk to a dead man,' he pleaded, 'will you bring this spirit up.?" "Are you trying to get me killed?" the woman demanded, You know that Saul had all of the mediums and fortune-tellers executed, you are spying on me." But Saul took a solemn oat that he wouldn't betray her.

Finally the woman said, 'Well whom do you want me to bring up.?

\"Bring me Samuel,' Saul replied.' When the woman saw Samuel, she screamed, you've deceived me! You are Saul."

\Don't be frightened!" The king told her, "What do you see.? "I see a specter coming up out of the grave" she said. He is an old man wrapped in a robe" Saul realized that it was Samuel and bowed low before him.

"Why have you distributed me by bringing me back." Samuel asked Saul. "Because I am in deep trouble' he replied. The philistine are at war with us and God has left me and won't reply by prophets or dreams; so I have called for you to ask you what to do." But Samuel tripled. "Why ask me if the God has left you and Has become your enemy.? He has done just as he said he would and have taken the kingdom from you and have given it to your rival, David All this has come upon you because you did not obey the Lord's instructions when he was so angry with Amalek. What's more, the entire Israel army will be routed and destroyed by the Philistines tomorrow, and you and your son's will be here with me."

The old man then looked at King, "The time that you have been asked to accomplish this mission, are some of the most difficult times in our existence. People in the church is more disobedient then in all creation since the dividing of Israel and Judah. I want to remind you of the times you are going through. The times, and space, and energy, of a universe suffering for disobedience. If it was possible taking this assignment twenty five years ago would have made today's assignment successful. Therious, this assignment may cause your life before it is complete. He wants me to share with you some things in general terms. Before him about twelve feet away in a tree limb was the raven, an eagle sat at the top of the tree and a dove swarmed down lightly to the ground next to the feet of the old man. There was nothing but silence. Two fresh graves, a stool, a tree, a raven, a dove, an eagle, time, air and an old man who had served God well. And he in his humble appearance stood on the other side of the grave.

He is here to support his good friend. God has allowed him privilege that most men never thought about.

The old man, far in years but not trembling, not even wrinkled, as steady as a rock. He appeared to be almost in a smile, but then he began to speak. "The power of Abaddon and Apollyon who are two of the same is just over the horizon, but even now you can witness the effect of their near presence, it is in the air, water, skies and under the earth. It won't be long before all of God's creation will come under huge earthquakes. Mountains will move out of their places, rivers will dry up and valleys will become as smooth as the desert in the fall of the year. Listen my son, let me tell you about the seven Trumpets; The trumpets will not blow until the seventh seal is opened. Six seals of God's wrath has already sounded, and now the seventh seal will bring forth the seven trumpets. This is a time when heaven shall be silent for half an hour, and then His wrath will bellow like a bull.

Trumpet #1. Hail and fire, mingled with blood was thrown upon the earth. And a third of the trees were burned up, and all green grass was burned up.

Trumpet #2. Something like a great mountain burning with fire was thrown into the sea, and a third of the sea became blood. And a third of the living creatures in the sea died, and a third of the ships were destroyed.

Trumpet #3. A great star fell from heaven, burning like a torch, and it fell on a third of the rivers and on the springs of waters. And on the springs of waters. The name of the star is Wormwood. A third of the waters became Wormwood, and many men died from the water, because it was made bitter.

The old man looked curiously at the young preacher and he felt sorry for young preachers throughout the land. The wind joined him, but now it was a distant red, mixed with green and yellow. The raven stood on one end of the grave and on the other end stood the dove, a white dove. Flying slowly overhead was an eagle, so slow that it seemed as if it would fall. It wings was wide, wider than any other eagle that he had saw. The old man looked at Braxton, that is what he called him when he wanted to get his attention. There were no room for smiles, for between now and then survival is the best that man can do. Then he continued on with his revelation of tomorrow's world.

Trumpet #4 At the sound of the fourth angel, A third of the sun was struck, a third of the moon,, and a third of the stars, so that a third of them were darken. A third of the day did not shine, and likewise the night. Preacher I heard a voice, Woe, woe, woe to the inhabitants of the earth, because of the remaining blasts of the trumpet of the three angels was about to sound.

Trumpet #5 I saw a star falling from heaven to earth. To him was given the key to the bottomless pit. And he opened the bottomless pit, and smoke arose out of the bottomless pit like the smoke of a great furnace, so the sun and the air was darken because of the smoke of the pit. Then out of the smoke locusts came upon the earth, and of them was given power, as the scorpions upon the earth has power. And they were not given authority to kill them, but to torment them for five months. Their torment was like the torment of a scorpion when he strikes a man, Son in those days men will seek death and not find it; they will desire to die,, and death will flee from them.

Trumpet #6 The four angels who were bound at the great river Euphrates were released. They had been prepared for the hour and day, month, (63) and year, were released to kill a third of mankind. These plagues, there were three of them killed a third of man kind.

The three plagues were fire, and the smoke and the brimstone which came out of their mouths.

Trumpet #7 Then the seventh angel sounded: And there were loud voices in heaven, saying, "The kingdom of this world have become the kingdoms of our Lord and of His Christ, and he shall reign forever and ever."

The old man cleared his throat looked at the grave, then he looked out into nowhere, and he whispered softly,

"Let not the wise man glory in his wisdom,
Let not the mighty man glory in his might,
Nor let the rich man glory in his riches;
But let him who glories glory in this.,
That he understands and knows me,
That I am the Lord, exercising loving kindness,
Judgment, and the righteousness in the earth.

They both heard the rumbling of thunder and saw the lightening flashing up against a dark cloud that appeared quicker than right now.

The rumbling did not carry with it the shaking of the earth. But the attention of souls knew that there was going to be a movement. The old man kind of looked as if he was about to get in a hurry. But he wanted to say some words of encouragement to the young man that had been his friend here on earth. Now he had wished that he did not have to see him, but he had been called up from the grave, called up for a purpose. Then he was going to go back, lie down and rest until that great getting up morning.

Son, there were a hesitation, I call upon you, by the mercies of God, to present your body to him, a living, consecrated sacrifice, well- pleasing to God--- for that is the only kind of worship which is truly spiritual. And do not shape your lives to meet the fleeting fashion of this world; but be transformed from it, by the renewal of your mind, until the very essence of your being is altered, so that, so that in your own life, you may prove that the will of God is good and well -pleasing and perfect. There were no good-by's or see you later. The man vanished away, the grave was gone, green grass stood all under the tree and down the little slope, but he still was not home. The place was pleasant and beautiful and soothing to look upon.

The sight of a young man's dream have come to an end.

Two things remained until his spirit released him from the second heaven. It was a journey to the third heaven where the Lord himself spoke to him in His son native language:

ابني، المهمة التي كنت على وشك أن تحمل سيكون لها تأثير إيجابي على جميع الكنائس في جميع أنحاء خلق بلدي. الناس الذين يعتقد أنهم اختيار لك، لم تفعل ذلك. كان قبولك يست لهم أن تعطي. هذه هي الفرصة الأخيرة للكنيسة الحق في الحصول عليه قبل عودة يسوع المسيح للكنيسة. فقد أصبحت التوافق، التي لا ترحم، والأخلاق هي مشكلة، حتى في المنبر، الكفر في الحرم هي لعبة لعبت على دماء يسوع المسيح. معاناته لا تعني شيئا لكثير من الناس الذين يقولون آمين إلى الحقيقة. لدي بعض الكلمات لأقول لك، وأنك لن تذكرها أو فهمها حتى يأتي ذلك الوقت.

الكلمات التي تسمع سوف يبدو غريبا لك، فلن يفهم منها، ولكن عندما حان الوقت، فإن التفاهم يكون هناك. وسوف تضع مرهم في روحك بالنسبة لك أن تعرف الشخص، وأنت لتحديد. ولكن الآن دعونا إعدادك لنجاح العام للرحلة.

ابني، وأنا سوف أعطيكم مكان من أي وقت مضى حيث كنت تطأ الروحي، والشعب الذي كنت قد أمر للإشراف. كما وعدت ابني، سوف أراضيكم تمتد من هنا إلى هناك. لا أحد سيكون قادرا على الوقوف ضد لكم كل أيام حياتك. كما كنت مع موسى والأنبياء، ولذا فإنني سوف أكون معكم؛ سأترك لكم أبدا أو يتخلى عنك. كن قويا وشجاعا، لأنك سوف يؤدي هؤلاء الناس لمتابعة كلمة الله القوية. كن قويا وشجاعا جدا، أن يكون حريصا على طاعة كل الشريعة التي أعطيت لك؛ لا يرجع عنه إلى اليمين أو إلى اليسار، والتي قد تكون ناجحة في أي مكان تذهب إليه. لا تدع هذا الكتاب من القانون تغادر من الفم جولة. التأمل فيه نهارا وليلا. بحيث قد يكون حريصا على ألا يفعل كل ما هو مكتوب فيه. فإنك سوف تكون مزدهرة وناجحة. أنا لم أمركم؟ كن قويا وشجاعا. لا يكون بالرعب. لا تثبط، لأن الرب إلهك يكون معك أينما ذهبت.

My son, the task that you are about to endure will have a positive effect upon all churches throughout my creation. The people who thought that they choose you, did not do so. Your acceptance was not theirs to give. This is the last chance for the church to get it right before Jesus Christ returns for the church. They have become compliancy, unforgiving, morality is a problem, even in the pulpit, unbelief in the sanctuary is a game played over the blood of Jesus Christ. His suffering does not mean anything to many of the people who say Amen to the truth. I have some words to say to you and you will not remember them or understand them until the time come.

The words that you hear will seem strange to you, you will not understand them, but when the time come, the understanding will be there. I will place an unction in your spirit for you to know the person, you are to select. But now let us prepare you for the overall success of the journey.

My son, I will give you ever place where you set your spiritual foot., and the people that you have been commanded to oversee. as I promised my son, Your territory will extend from here to there. No one will be able to stand up against you all the days of your life. As I was with Moses and the prophets, so I will be with you.; I will never leave you or forsake you.

Be strong and courageous, because you will lead these people to follow the mighty word of God. Be strong and very courageous, be careful to obey all the law that I have given you.; do not turn from it to the right or to the left, that you may be successful wherever you go. Do not let this book of the law depart from tour mouth; meditate on it day and night. So that you may be careful to do everything written in it. Then you will be prosperous and successful. Have I not commanded you? Be strong and courageous. Do not be terrified; do not be discouraged, for the Lord your God will be with you wherever you go.

He could not understand the language. But he knew that it was coming from the throne of God. He was in a place that was too beautiful for man to imagine. When the language stop flowing, he still did not understand his position in its existence. But a forward flowing spirit took him by the reigns of his mind and tough his spirit, he could feel himself moving downward, And then, there he was, somewhat relaxes in his easy chair, back in his office, in the house that he called home, the one that God had given to him that he did not earn. In this location he has a wife and three kids, a cat that resemble a rabbit, he had never noticed the resemble before. This was the only thing that had reminded him of the trip that he could hardly believe. He now wondered if he should tell anyone, no one would believe him. He thought for a moment, how he would tell some of his close friends; he tried to recall the trip, he could only remember the old man, and that may have been because there was a picture of his friend on the mental.

There he sat in his easy chair in disbelief, and he did not know what he did not believe. The trip to the second heaven cleared up many things for now. He had a feeling that for the time being, he knew what he needed to know. He sat there not knowing what to do next. He couldn't even imagine as to what to think about, or what he needed to have on his mind.. His mind was not blank, it was not empty, it was not void, it was without understanding. The young man found himself void of movement and for the first time there was throbbing fear, almost as if he feared to move. For a moment fear and doubt creped in un invited and unwanted. But when he gave up trying, a peace and a calm joined by righteous joy released him to move about. (on)There was no time to do nothing, he had to put his plan into operation. And he knew that it would have to start with some on his enemies list. Now he knew what he did not know at first. That he was put into this position by man to fail. They knew that he would do enough, so that when they relieved him, the group that they would insert into that position would succeed. But then God has assured him that if he was faithful to his father and maintained a strong faith in his son Jesus Christ he would succeed.

CHAPTER #7

Time of challenge

(If any of you lack wisdom, let him ask of God, that
giveth to all men liberally, and upbraideth nor; and
it shall be given him.) (James1:5)

Today had been a heavy day, much had gone on, that filled his
head with wisdom and knowledge far above his understanding. He
wanted to take a short trip to a out of the way place of beauty and
water, nothing but the sound of water hitting the bank of the earth,
The darkness of the shadow of the tree limbs kept flirting with the
water and the bank of the lake. He had driven approximately thirty
to forty five minutes from the city, turned off onto a dusty road
and in minutes he was there. It was like a fresh breath of air that
made him feel like a real man. He did not get out of his car, he just
observed the water, hill sides, small valleys and the green grass and
tree leaves that sat so proudly in its place
  Thirty minutes later he woke up, his mind was clear. He took
out a couple of good writing pens and two secretary pads. Where do
I start from, he said to himself, the beginning was too far back. The
beginning and the starting place had some of the same characters.
The starting place would provide him some still alive preachers to
help assist the journey. He would not tell them about last night, he
would only tell them about what they already knew. And ask their

opinion, to get the information that he needed. He would need some of the older war horses, many who had retired, some in nursing homes, there were some who was alive but could not communicate.

While he was sitting there, he remembered an elderly pastor who did not like visitors, but would talk on the phone all day. He loved to talk about those good old days, back in the day. His name was (Ray Hinton)He looked at his watch and saw that it past time for him to get up and take a walk. He called him and his wife answered the phone. She was glad to hear from pastor King, she said that the senior pastor was not in the best of mood. The few people that has called, seldom call because he always wanted to talk about back in the day. How they use to do it, and he has been critical of the young preachers. Rev. he is getting hard to live with. She informed him that the pastor need to be wanted. She had tried to get him to retire when he had reached eighty years old,, now four years later he is just hanging in there. She said to the young pastor, if he could find something to do that he enjoy doing, the both of us would be a happy family. She went on to say that he is too old to get involved in any activity. She said that he likes driving, being out by himself. Then she said, "You may not believe this but daddy likes to meet people and talk with them about the good news. Not at home, I never understood his reasons or motive. Rev. I want you to know how much we appreciate your friendship and kindness over the years. He always talks about you. By the way, congratulation for being chosen as moderator of the Cap/ Rock District Association to lead them back to health. Our prayer goes up for you.

Do you have time to talk with him for a while? Any way let me get him.

Remember you can't talk too long, because the longer you talk, the less that I have to put up with. They both got a laugh out of that comment. When the young man spoke to the pastor, he found out that pastor was disappointed with the D.A. and he thought that they had done him terrible wrong. They had dropped him, from his point of view, for no reason at all. But when King calmed him down, they began to talk earnestly about current events that will affect the church. Finally the old man cleared his throat.

"What is it that you want me to do." The young man said, "Let me be honest with you, I need you to help me from under cover, to build the city brotherhood, to assist us in building the district, state, and national gathering of mature saved men."

There was a long hesitation between the two men., The old man could not believe what he was hearing. Finally they need me, he said to himself. But they need me at a time when I an old. Then he hesitated in thought- But I'm not dead yet. I know that God will give me the strength to fulfill their desires for my service. "Pastor King " he said with a smile, what you have said is a mouth full. Your words excitement me, it bring back life to an old man's soul. Rev. King spoke slowly, there were something about this conversation that puzzled Pastor Ray Hinton. There were something that he did not understand. He understood that the young man needed help, he also understood that the young man needed his help. But for him to help it would take more than him to even start this project. He wondered if, if, if he wanted him to step down from Pastor. His mind was running wild, but when he thought about the city=district-state and maybe the national. He knew that if he had to do all of that he would have to step down. That would be exactly what his wife wanted him to do.

All of a sudden it did not seem like a bad idea. But he did not know where the idea came from. He and his wife have been at odds for some time about him stepping down from the church. They both knew that his son was ready, willing, and able to take over the church. If the truth was known, the membership was also ready, but with respect to him, they stood behind him. He and his wife was set financially, he did not need the church to live on. He had social security, retirement from the Army, retirement from the post office, and he had a little business of fixing lawn mowers that supported he and his wife. He thought for another moment, wandering where this idea came from. Then he informed the young preacher that his wife was cooking and it would be ready by seven thirty. He chuckled. Son come on over, bring your wife to keep my wife company, we will see what the Lord have to say about this business.

Rev. King called to his wife and informed her that they were going over for dinner. Pastor Hinton's wife could not believe what she was hearing. She came to the door and looked at him. "Did I understand you to say that someone was coming over for dinner" He did not respond to her question/. Prepare the guest room, they may be spending the night."

Then he turned to face her, "By morning we will know if you will get your wish. Our friend has assignment that he has not understood the magnitude nor the depth. I'm going to spend some time in prayer, you see, he is not the only one who does not grasp the total importance of this assignment, if he remain true to God ... ... only God knows what the outcome will be.

The young preacher, who pastor's a church in the community arrived approximately later that evening, trying to figure out why Rev. Hinton asked him over for this conference, and dinner, when everyone knew that he did not invite people over to his house. An unction of the Lord informed him that this would be his first disciple, and that Rev. King would make a decision soon that would shock the Christian community. His intentions were not to shock the community, but to prepare to rebuild lives that lived in the community. What could the father tell Hinton that he understood more than the young man could not understand. What could he know on earth, that the young man was wrestled with in the second heaven. He thought for a moment, no one know about the visit to the second heaven. If the fact was known, he had forgotten about the visit and what was said. Yes, he knew then that the spirit that was all alone had informed him that this was his first disciple.

That evening when the two families had made their pleasant greetings, all but Rev. King was surprise and a little shocked. It was not a relaxed time of the evening, but there were no enemies in the room. Matter of fact no one asked the visitors to sit down, and it did not seem as if the young couple was looking for a place to set. Rev. Hinton soon became estatic with Jesus joy. Something about this meeting had the old pastor walking on cloud nine.. He never thought that this element in his life would show up before death. At eighty four years and a reasonable good health, God had blessed him beyond his asking. After the hello's had been said, they just kind of looked at each other. The old man was the first to confess that this was the happiest day of his life. He went on to say that he did not know why he felt so joyful, why today was so wonderful, he just grabbed his wife and hugged her. The young man felt a Godley fear, that the Lord's hand was moving in their lives. There was an uneasy chuckled throughout the four of them. It was like, they had not been here before; As if something was coming to bear and they could not stop its approach. A quick observation of the clock on the wall screamed out to all who would listen, that it was a little (after four o'clock on a Saturday evening). But then it did not take the wife long to whip up a meal.

When the two pastors entered the room through the door, the air had stretched across the floor inside the door and they had to walk over it to enter his office. It was different now than before; before the air was in a ball like shape. Today it was in bright colors- green, blue, dark brown with a slender streak of pale black. The old man finally asked King to sit down, then he spoke as if he was looking into a land on the other side of something. King, he said, "black people who lives in the Aquifer-Ogallala which lies beneath eight states from South Dakota to Texas, is the life blood of one of the world's most productive farming economies. The aquifer also known as the Ogallala, makes possible a large share of the country's output of corn, wheat, and cattle.` The water level which caused these and other product's to flourish in year's past have become severely depleted.

Churches that make up this area have dwindled down to 10 to 20 members. The majority of these members work in low paying jobs, mostly on the farm. Soon the people who lives in these area's will not have any where to go, their skills are inadequate for today's skill jobs level. The church must find a way for these peoples to survive. The sad part about this whole thing, is without help (where) help is not affordable). People will find themselves looking for a way to die, when there is no food in the trash cans. The church should be able to help people with salvation, regardless of the condition of the world. It may be that (salvation not survival) will have the greatest need in the lives of the people in this area. If the Church does not get ready now, putting people and resources of all kind in places where they can respond; We will lose thousand of people who does not know any better. When the wells dry up and the rain stop coming and the pipeline become too expensive to share water. The church must be in place until Christ return for the waiting congregation. Leaders must remind themselves as leader and role models that we are on the apron of His return. When food get critically low or run out it may be too late to tell a dying person about salvation when they want to survive.

King looked at the old man, he had never heard him talk like this before. He had almost forgot what reason that he was here to fulfill. My God, he said to himself, I never heard any of the pastors express their concern for our survival in the near future.

He kept looking at the old man after he had sat down. All of a sudden, he did not look old, he appeared as a vibrant warrior that he had never been before. The glow that came leaping out of his spirit, was an encouragement to the trip before them. He kind of leaned over in a ball, and quickly thanked God for a tremendous beginning. He saw confidence in himself and the old man, they had began to move into the right direction.

The floor had become black and white squares. Where did these squares come from? He knew for sure they were not there when they walked into the room. But it seem as if the old man did not notice them. There were no squares where they were sitting, and there were a small area between them and the squares, which was the natural floor. The air had circled the area where there were no squares. They were surrounded by the air, and now the air showed all of the colors in the universe, it was a beauty to behold. The raven was there joined by a (peacock). The (Raven) was solid black or sometime blue. The (eagle) shifted from somewhere to the other side of the sacred area. The eagle seem to be different, he seem to have a mind, he seem to be thinking, then he turned his head away toward the door. The (rabbit) seem to be hiding beneath a small tree, but the tree was not there, it never was because there were no place for it to grow. The buzzard was not present, but the thought of the buzzard was present. The thought of him not being presence, left the room a pleasant place to be.

"Young man where do we start. I do not know where the beginning originated. I do not want to guess, I want to know the facts. I've heard that you were chosen to fail and that already have a group of men to take over when it becomes apparent that you cannot take the district any further. They will believe that you can set a solid foundation, with people in places. They are going to make sure that you fail, maybe fail is not the word. They want you to become frustrated and step down. Son I am here for the long haul, whatever time that God gives me, here is where I want to be. Son I just wanted you to hear it from the outside. I don't want you to think that the governing body is behind you. That they will do every thing possible to help you succeed. Those smiles and pats on the back, and them calling you their friend; be careful, there is a trap for you. But God is able and willing. They chose you to fail, but God has chosen you to succeed. Only your disobedience, pride, and thinking you are more than who you are can release God from your protection.

Meanwhile as the women sat around the breakfast table, it showed how happy they were being together. They were overjoyed to spend time together without being in a hurry. They both took a deep breath and then laugh out loud. But soon the laughter was gone and a more serious face appeared. (Jan), You are the only person that I can share this with. When my husband and I got married, I was so exciting to be in his company. He was dashing, exciting had money, good looking. I saw him as he was and not what he was going to become. A few years ago I lost my love for him, and then came the time I did not want to be around him. But I was the pastors wife, I had to play the game. When we came home we did not pretend, we was honest with each other. He knew that I did not love him anymore, and I discovered that he never loved me; he was just excited by the way that I was built and looked. We made the most of it, and here we are."

"He stopped people from coming to the house, because he thought that people would see through the smoke screen we were putting up. With all honestly in the later years he had become to dislike pasturing a church. I had hoped for some time that he would find another interest. When we heard that your husband had been asked to head up the Cap /Rock District Association, I prayed earnestly that new life would be pumped back into him. I don't know how much longer I can put up with this stagnated relationship. Look at him he is excited, because this is his last change and he knows that he will do a good job. If this work, it is going to help every person that touches this program. Then she laugh. I don't even know what the program is, it has not been revealed. This program has got to work, it just may save our unhappy marriage.

Sister King dropped her head and looked at the floor. She wanted to say something, but she held it back. Neither woman said a word for some time, then sis. King spoke, "If I can understand a small part of what is going on, my husband will be force to make a drastic change in the district. It is not that he can't do it, but I don't know if he has ever practice total obedience that God requires. Oh, I hope I'm not saying this the wrong way. My husband has in the past interpreted the scripture liberally. So much so that it distorts the meaning of God's word to believers. He has searched for sound that makes people shout and happy. His meaning is short on eternal life, and there is not enough substance to drive home the meaning that God intended. If God takes control, he certainly has the right two men."

The other lady said, "You have to have something to give up.

Something that is dear to you. Something that you want to keep, but realize that in giving you are the better person."

Sister King had become uncomfortable in the company of Fay Hinton the old man's wife. She looked at Fay and Fay looked nervous, as if something important was bothering her. Finally sis. King gave her permission to share her deepest secrets. She informed sis. King that her husband had killed his brother over a crap game. This incident hurt his mother and father so bad that they threw him out of the house.. He hated them for that, and to this day, even though they are dead, he hates them. God is not pleased, but he has allowed him to pastor all these years. My husband is tormented by the killing of his brother and his hate for his parents. He need a one time repentance activity, where he can give up and let God. She went on to say, "I pray God that this may be his last chance for spiritual survival.:

Rev. King un-crossed his legs, leaned back in the comfortable chair. King was a small thin man of distinctions, the old man was tall, he did not have much of a smile, but a look that made you pay attention. They were kind of like the odd couples. They did not look to be friendly servants, but they were God chosen. The wife came in and asked if they wanted coffee. The tall slender man informed his wife to set the coffee pot-hooked up and two coffee cups. Then he smiled at her, please close the door gently, and the two of you take some time to pray for this visit.

Rev. King, looked at Pastor. Hinton, "Where do you think that the demise of the church has found its way to the door of hell. I know we can always go back to sin; but there is something more human that is pulling the church apart. There is something that we are doing or not doing, that is causing the church to walk differently than what God intended. It's the church inability to read and study God's word, then keep it with the help of God. The church has refused to be obedient to God. They give one excuse after another, they talk about what other people are saying and how they see the situation. They listen to hear what man says about God's word. They do not contact God about the core activity of their lives. They look for a different way home, a way that is comfortable to them.

They want the best living of this world and then eternal life in the world to come.

I see a wide spread followers of a belief that once saved is always saved. They take this to mean that once a person have been saved, regardless as to how long ago; it does not matter what he has gone through, how much sin he has done, how much disobedience he has been involved it, how much disrespect he has shown to God, and his house. He may even have walked away from the straight and narrow and joined the wide road to destruction, have lived a life that a rank sinner would not live. And yet believe that he is still saved. Eternal salvation, is indeed a true statement. No man can take you away from God while you desire to stay in the shadow of the almighty. If you choose to walk away, that is your privilege, that is your choice as free moral agents. but no one can take you away from God. There are many in the churches who think that they are saved, because they have become emotional in a worship service, they will shout, try and give God praises for their high emotional feeling. But that does not mean that they are saved. If you are going to teach eternal salvation or once saved, always saved-you should allow God to give you what to say to the person that is in front of you.

If God has not convinced you that the person is saved, don't use the term, once saved always saved. You don't want the person to think he is saved, when he is not. Because if he thinks that he is saved by what you are saying, and he is not, he is hell bound. If you are going to use the term there should be three people who are in agreement; God the life giver, the person who desire salvation and you who want to give the person in front of you an opportunity to accept Jesus Christ or reject Him. Just make sure that he is saved if you are going to use that term.

In the book of (Ezekiel 33:12-16 NIV) "Therefore, son of man, say to your countrymen. 'The righteousness of the righteous man will not save him when he disobey, and the wickedness of the wicked man will nor cause him to fall when he turns from it. The righteous man, if he sins, will not be allowed to live because of his former righteousness. If I tell the righteous man that he will surely live, but then he trust in his righteousness and does evil, none of the righteous things he has done will be remembered; He will die for the evil he has done.. And if I say to the wicked man, you will surely die, but then he turns away from his sin and does what is just and right---if he gives back what he took in pledges for a loan, return what he has stolen, follow the decree that gives life, and does no evil, he will surely live, he will not die. None of the sins he has committed will be remembered against him. He has done what is just and right, he will surely live.

There are some that teach homosexual is just another sin, that it is a way of life and that God understands when he made man, that some would be like they are. Some teach that once saved is always saved no matter what kind of life you live. Others teach that one can have as many women as he can take care of, drink his fill of liquor to help keep him happy. That it is o.k. to beat his wife as long as he does not take her life or leave her maimed. That she need whipping every once and a while, so that she will know who the boss is. Drugs have their place in man's society they say, it help him beat the difficulty of living. Give him confidence in the bed room and the cooperate office. There are other attitudes in the Christian church, that is against the word of God. But when a Christian has lost their first love, and have determined that they don't need God as grand mother and grand father once did. We have come to believe that living on both sides of the world, doing basically what we want to do, hoping that we are going to get to heaven, coupled with going to church on a fairly regular basis is enough to enjoy eternal salvation and at the end, eternal life.

It is a terrible thing to talk of God abandoning anyone. And yet there are two reasons for that. 'God give man free will, and he respect that free will. In the last analysis not even he can interfere with it. In Ephesians (4:19) Paul speak of men who have abandoned themselves to lasciviousness; they have surrendered their whole will to the influence of Satan. Hosea (4:17) has this terrible sentence: Ephraim is joined to idols; let him alone. Before man there stand an open choice; and it has to be so. Without choice there can be no goodness. And without choice there can be no love. A coerced goodness is not real goodness; and a coerced love is not love at all. If men deliberately choose to turn their backs on God after he has sent his son Jesus Christ into the world, not even he can do anything about it.

And yet in this word abandonment there is more to it then previously discussed--there is judgment. It is one of the grim facts of life that the more a man sin the easier it is to sin. He may began with a kind of shuttering awareness of what he is doing, and end by sinning without a second thought of remorse. It is not that God is punishing him; he is bringing punishment upon himself. And steadily making himself the slave of sin. The conse --quence and punishment of sin, is in the sin, God does not have to punish us for doing wrong. The sin, the wrong, the mistake, the error carries its own consequence.

The most terrible thing about sin is this power to beget sin. It is the awful responsibility of free-will that It can be used in such a way that in the end it is obligated and a man becomes the slave to sin, self-abandoned to the wrong way. And sin is always a lie, because the sinner thinks that it will make him happy, whereas in the end it ruins life, both for himself and for others, in this world and in the world to come.

"Pastor King ", he said getting to his feet, "I saw a book written by one of the brotherhood brothers in our district association. There is not a book printed that can match that book. It goes inside and pluck at the heart of believers. The title of this book is, "The Brother Up Next" It takes the believing brother from the respect for God's ownership in our finance, to the three ways of giving. It teaches the believing brother that God owns it all. And the book end with conflict resolution. We want to teach each brother in our district how to study, read and apply this marvelous book. We want to get with the writer and publisher of the book, so that we can make it available to all the men in the district. We want them to know what every brother in this district association believe. They can carry this book home with them and keep a copy in their car. It is a good book for the husband and wife to study together. It help lay the foundation that if we are poorer than we should be, the responsibility lie with the brother. God's word gives us the price we need to pay, condition that we have to meet. And the strength of our asking. If we can get the men to commit to this fine book, we can go to the state president with out success and I believe that he will back this movement.

King kind of chuckled, "I never knew that you felt this way about the makeup of our association. I never heard you say anything in our meetings that was against what was discussed. How long have you thought this way." Hinton kind of smiled, "I know that I asked you for your plan, and I have not stopped talking yet. There is one other thing that I would like to share. This is a little touchy, but I did not have anyone to try it out on." Rev. King was getting a little uneasy because he was now ready to share his plan. This meeting for discussion was designed for this purpose; but he bowed his head for Hinton to go on. Dr. uh, there is something in our make up that challenges us to be defeated, in an area that we must succeed.."

He went on to share how that God's promises, blessings and financial awareness come together to relieve the Christian of their inability to be without. There is no need for Christian's to be believers and at the same time be without. There is something on the side of Christianity that pulls negatively against out ability to succeed. He went on to say that we must balance faith, believing and financial awareness to a successful blend. Christian people defeat themselves. God's word give them every chance to move off the floor of always scuffling, barely having enough to survive. A mindset and attitude change must be taught in the churches, where people will believe God's word. Look at Joshua 1:7-9, follow this pattern that God has set in this universe for us, with John 15:1-17 of the new Testament.

It plainly shares with us what we have to do, and when we have completed the condition that God requires, we can have whatever we ask for in the spirit.

He went on to say that Christians must be re-conditioned to believe that all things are possible to those who truly believe. They must understand that Christ paid a price for our salvation, Not only did he suffer but he gave his innocent life. If we are to reap the benefits of an all mighty God, we must pay the price and meet the conditions. Some time when we read the word of God it seem hard to us, yet, with God's help we can obtain his offering from glory. Look at just one verse, if you fully understood this verse, believed that God would be true to his word, you can have what ever you ask for. (John 15:7niv) " If you remain in me and my words remain in you, ask whatever you wish, and it will be given you. This is my Fathers glory, that you bear much fruit, showing yourself to being my disciple."

He turned and looked at a picture of Marian Anderson and Dr. Ralph Bunch hung on his wall. He reached out and re-positioned them back the way they were at first. We must find a way to help people better themselves and they do not know what they are doing. He turned around with his head half bent to the side. When you look at Christianity, the overall scene of things. At first you only see two that would interest a lost soul; ever lasting life and survival on this earth. We have not done a good job balancing the two, so that the man and woman will have something to go alone with their suffering. Most of the church's giving come from the aged and people just trying to make it. We need to give these people a financial joy to thank God about. There is no need to have poor people in church, they are there

because we have not taught them properly. We have not taught them because we are not sure ourselves how the catch 22 goes in this matter. God want to teach us, but we have not been willing to learn. Now we must, it's too late to give excuses of his mind. for there is no reason to continue to fail God's people, begging them for their little money, then go to the house with green back in out pocked.

He confessed that he was not sure how to do it, but admitter that it must be done, and they will have to figure out a way that matches the will of God to get it accomplished. He thought for a while as if he was waiting for more wisdom and knowledge that seem to have gotten lost in the equation of his mind. Finally he gave up, took his seat and raised both hands for Rev. King to go on. They both smiled, for by now they were not sure where to start. But time was limited, Christ return for the church was drawing closed than it ever have been before. They talked about how the association got into this mess. It did not happen overnight, or even yesterday. The shambles that the association is in, so is the church. You cannot separated one demise from another. King said, I remember something that my professor said when I was in school.

He said, Living in a global village of Western society, today's society, today's listeners, both young and old, have a familiarity with elements of the Christian faith that has bought about a contempt ... ... Western civilization wallows in fragments of Christian clichés and paraphernalia. This saturation reduces Christianity to slogans and meaningless phrases. Many people consider Christianity old hat. This sad truth has given rise to multitudes of people who are wondering through life with little meaning or fulfillment. The passages of the Bible has been so watered down in some circles that it has no relevance to what people face in real life.

Real life situation is in the gut where we live, sleep, eat and have our being. If everyday life become frustrated in our attempt to survive, to live, to progress, and prepare to die. If preparing to leave this world for a better place, requires that we learn how to live closer to God, where will we find out basic training. The place we learn how to live in a world of excitement, fun, success and financial responsibility. All of these are offered from the Bible, they are promised, they are God's way of blessing us for our obedience. But obedience can be a problem with the church. Man does nor desire the walk with an almighty God as he once did; now he drags part of the world with him when he walks into the church. His conversation is not about living Holy, it is about survival and doing what we want to do about getting ahead. Man want to do the less that he can for his entrance into the kingdom. The less that man does is not enough to fulfill the desires of God. Doing the less, or just enough, that you think that you can to survive is not enough for God's accommodation. God need dedicated souls who are committee to the word and will of God. We all at one time or the other owe God a debt for committing to be obedient to His word.

We cannot put the demise of the church in one corner or the other. The leaders was at the church before the association ever existed. The pastors attitude, mindset and motive existed before we can remember. There was a time when pastors were concerned for the membership, but did not know to teach them financial freedom. Now as many of the local pastors return to the walk of Jesus Christ. Realizing that their walk in the shadow of the Lord will not hold up for them to receive everlasting life. It only takes a few to make the decision, that I'm going to do it His way, regardless of what the cost is. Others will see them, and after a while, they to will follow the direction that God has laid out for man to follow.

Rev. King said, "I remember when our association took a dive, without a thought of returning to where they had left from. It was at a meeting near an airport. When the churches who had paid their dues was called, it was less than expected. When the churches who did not represent was called; it was the recommendation that they would be removed from the book.." They went on to talk about the failure of the group, what the remaining group could do. They forgot that there were not enough churches to support the district and State convention. What they should have done, they must do now.

CHAPTER #8

It all belong to him

"And he spake a parable unto them to this end, that
me ought to always pray and not to faint." (Luke 18:1.)

There is a strange combination of mind, spirit, and soul that must
come together at the same time. They must come together without
being consciously ware that each exist. Every thing that a Christian
does from praying to God, to shaking hands, to living Holy under
a righteous loving intent to please God. More than anything else,
we need to live Holy to the point that God has made us aware that
He owns it all. If indeed he owns it all, then he can give us what
he desires and will never run out of money. Holy living and being
obedient to God and His word; living a daily life that is totally
controlled by our loving father, This must be our goal; not to let
Satan interfere with what he has given us. Being a mature Christian
will lift the believer above the deadly sin of the flesh. It will put him
on the narrow road that bring blessings and promises to the heart
and soul of the believer.

The mature Christian must bring together the best that God has
with the best promises and blessings that he can afford to give. The
bible is saturated with what God will do, if we meet the condition
that God require. There is absolutely nothing that is out of reach of
our heavenly father. He has promised us that we cannot out give him

of what he owns. We must be mindful of the power of God to give to his obedient children. Nothing stands outside of his power. Look at (Eph. 3:20,niv) "Now to him who is able to do immeasurably more than all we ask or imagine, according to his power that is at work within us." We must call upon all resources that is available to us. Every day we must be mindful of the power of God working within us. To rebuild this association, to put it back to where people respect it and the people who are in charge, we must use every once of God's help that he will in-trust us with.

Look at 11 King 20:1-6 NIV. "In those days Hezekiah became ill and was at the point of death. The prophet Isaiah son of Amoz went to him and said, this is what the Lord says: Put your house in order, because you are going to die; you will not recover.

\Hezekiah turned his face to the wall and prayed to the Lord. Remember O Lord, how I have walked before you faithfully and with wholehearted devotion and have done what is good in your eyes, and Hezekiah wept bitterly.

\Before Isaiah had had left the middle court, the word of the Lord came to him, Go back and tell Hezekiah, the leader of my people. This is what the Lord, The God of your father David, says: I have heard your prayers and seen your tears; I will heal you. On the third day from now you will go up to the temple of the Lord. I will add fifteen years to your life. And I will deliver you and this city from the hands of the Assyria. I will defend this city for my sake and for the sake of my servant David."

This is not only a prophet sharing a message, this is God himself sending a message that come directly from heaven. It does not come from the flesh, but from the heart of heaven above. He is telling his servant, that he is going to die. The sickness that has brought Hezekiah to his knees more than once, this sickness God will not cure, the servant will have to prepare himself for death. The servant did not take God's word for his death; he went on his knees and faced the wall. It is here that he reminded God of his faithfulness and his obedience to Jehovah God. He cried out with the help of

God himself, and he spared him fifteen more years. When a servant on his knees and in tears cry out to God. If he can get God to have compassion on him or his situation, God will deliver him.

If Rev. King can get and train those people God's way of doing things, we can raise this association past the level where it once was. Unconscious, Everything that we do for God, there should be an expectation of accomplishment, and financial fulfillment. We are to believe and patiently expect that God will give more to us than we can give to him. We must truly believe that if we make sacrifices to please God in all ways. We will soon see that he has already been there. Had laid the foundation of prosperity in the road that we travel.

He knows from being God what road we are going to travel. He even knows before hand of our obedience to his perfect will. The power of our believing that God is true to his word is not easy, it is a difficult journey that is paved with financial pit falls as well as ripe to ready fruit, that is there for the asking.

Rev. King went back to talking about what caused the association demise. The failure of one generation after another generation, one failure after another until they did not know where to get the strength to build an adequate foundation to stand on. The people in the association failed themselves and the foundation. And when they went back into the churches they could do nothing but fail those who God had chosen them to protect. They covered their heads with a wet blankets of lies, to themselves, their families and the church. They did not want to hear the words and laughter, from a people outside the church. But looking with open eyes at the disappointment that had slowly crept into the hearts of the saints that God loved; was absolutely heart breaking. One generation had failed on purpose, reaching for things that did not belong to them. And the next did not know which way to go. Did not know where to look for direction, so they fell in line with the past generation. Accepting the wisdom of the streets, and the parking lot, failing to turn to God for his wisdom and understanding.

He could not help wondering if there had been something that he could have done. But he thought to himself that his life style was not far from the way of life of those in past generations who had failed God's people. The fact of the matter, those churches that was cut off, on that miserable night at the end of the summer; were aware that they had not paid what they had promised. Some of them did not have the money, others were disappointed as to how the association was run. Some of the smaller churches wanted more leadership teaching, given to their pastor and deacons, and Sunday school teachers. But the group did not take time to check with each church to see if they could help them in any way. The group had become so self willed into themselves that they did not care. They no longer cared about people, they cared about money and power. They had moved away from being concern for people, what happen to them. They never talked to God as a group as what to do with those they had dismissed. They never even contacted them to inform them about their action.

Be reminded that some of the pastors were sitting in the room and they were cut loose because they did not pay their money. He knew that under his leadership that will never happen again. He knew that he had to show a message, talk a message, live a message. He knew then that on Saturdays evenings he had to choose a community and just walk around and talk to people; not about anything special, just talk about the Lord and His desires for our life.

He was there that night, he knew that the love of God had forgotten to flow that night. It seem as if they did not want God present, for they had made up in their mind what they were going to do.. When we are confronted with doing things God's way or what we think is right; if we are not careful we will choose what we think is right. Many pastors of yesterdays association have lost their first love. They are now riding on the promises of the air that have no direction, it is blowing to handle needs. Hurt pastors, hurt membership, strained relationship between brothers of the cloth, who preach on Sunday morning, pray for man's soul upon asking, give direction that is suppose to come from God.

He stopped for a moment, his face drawn in disappointment, and thought's of Jeremiah 6:16-21. Filled his mind to the brim. He went to the inside coat pocket and pulled out his small Bible. He went to Jer. The sixth chapter. He could not remember it by heart, so he read it from the living Bible. "Yet the Lord pleads with you still; ask where the good road is, the Godly path you used to walk in, in the days off long ago. Travel there, and you will find rest for your souls. BUT YOU REPLIED,NO!, that is not the road we want! I set watchman over you to warn you ; listen for the sound of the trumpet! It will let you know when trouble comes. BUT YOU SAID, NO! We won't pay any attention!

\This, then, is my decree against my people: Listen to it, distant lands, listen to it, all the earth. I will bring evil upon this people! It will be the fruit of their own sin, because they will not listen to me. I will make an obstacle course of the pathway of my people, fathers and sons will be frustrated; neighbor and friends shall collapse together." The association is in a terrible mess, but God is stronger than all of those he has created. But he can't help us if we say no to his direction. How can he help us if we stand off stiff-necked, in disobedience, rebelling against the all powerful God Surely the leaders of the association, knew that they were going against the word of God.

Rev. King went on to say, before we can correct what have been done, we must find the people to put at the wheel. He wanted Ray Hinton to find another strong brother or pastor, or preacher, who have the time to give to this journey. (That person will be his assistant.)He will have to believe that God is who he is, and his word stands for the reality of life. How to chose this person is a responsibility of Rev. King and Rev. Hinton, but if God does not wrap himself around their total being, the task will never be completed. They both are aware that God is the one that is choosing the men for the task. But without the man surrendering he cannot be used. We cannot spend too much time trying to figure out how God does things. There are things that he does that we do not understand. But an understanding is not a condition of God's word, but having faith in Jesus Christ IS.

Rev. Hinton rose to his feet, age had taken it's toll on his legs, they were a little weak and unsteady. "I will travel from church to church and prayer meeting to prayer meeting, and then to brotherhood and to the porch of unknown men for observation. At the end of three months, six if it has to be; I will record names that I feel that the Lord has shown me. After I record their names, I will go back to them, and in general terms talk to them about the depth of God. How can it be possible for a man to be totally surrendered to God and still live in a world of sin. Can man live so close to God that God will respond to the prayers of his children. Respond by sharing with him those things that he ask for to help build the association.

Rev. King began to feel restless. His face changed as if something was about to come over him. He looked around the room, and it looked strange to him. The black and white blocks that had covered the floor, had vanished into thin air. There were no signs of the animals, just the doves was flying away. They flew as if that had accomplished a mission of mercy. Finally the dove looked back, He is the last anything that was in the room except the two men. Hinton looked for his pipe, but something was on his mind. But at this time it had not cleared his mind, he was gently wrestling with his thoughts when it settled in for a stay.

The book that we were talking about, the brother up next. Do you know where the author can be contacted, what state does he live." Rev. King thought for a moment. He opened his satchel and pulled out a copy of brother up next. Not only does he live in Texas, he is a member of this association. Rev. King was looking at Hinton intensely. What do you have on your mind. Hinton had never met the author. Do not remember the two of them talking about him. But it goes to reason that the author of this book, is the kind of brother you want to build your foundation on. Surely, there is something about who he is, meets God's qualifications for this task.

The brother is a little aggressive, King went on to say, " he is just like a bull dog, when he gets holt of something he will never let it go. He is a structured person that many people in the Texas convention does not like. Some do not know why they don't like him. One thing is what ever he is talking about, he know his subject. I have to admit that he knows how to build this association, but whether or not you can get enough people to work with him is another question. If you are thinking about using him, keep him in the background. Do not let him lead out. You can call on him to answer questions, call upon him to stand in another person place. He does his best work from under cover. He is not a people person, people are uncomfortable with his presence. With all honesty he has a mean streak and look that cause people to be uneasy in his presence.

Ray, the first thing that we have to produce is an organizational chart of the D.A. This chart keeps all persons concern, informed as to where the program is at all times. The cost and the time of completion, in this case the structure and what is to be learned that makes it better than the one before. Holmes is the brothers name, he is also the author of the book. He is close to an expert as such, when it comes to the organization chart. I have to admit that I'm not sure what the chart is all about. He and I have talked about this chart, and all that I know, I got from him. To be honest with you, there is much about it that I do not understand. And until now it did not concern me. I've always thought that as long as you stay with the bible, one could not go wrong. But now I know what it is like to need it and don't have the slightest idea of how to put it together. You have to make it plain to him what you want him to do, and what the association intend to do, and how it is to effect the community. Then get out of the way and let him work. This is your man, before you talk with any of the dropped churches, let him put together a structured program to build the association. One other thing, he will ask you if you have a vision from the Lord. If you can convince him that you heard from heaven; he will put together the plan. The PLAN and the VISION will results in a GOAL to build the convention on the foundation of the heavenly father wishes. Then slowly he repeated the three steps. Vision from God, plan developed by a friend of Jesus, and goals accepted by leadership.

They looked at each other and knew that they were on their way. It was getting close to sundown and the rain that had been forecasted, began to come in sheets, then came hale, and then came the 60-65 miles an hour winds. The electric went off and Mrs. Hinton brought out the candles. They all gathered around the small table. Each one laid his or hand upon their own bible. It was an agreed thing for all of them to be quiet and pray God for protection. It did not last a long time, by seven that evening it had stopped, and the (FALL) sun had reappeared.

Rev. King motioned to Rev. Hinton if he could use the phone. The old man bowed his head, Yes. Braxton picked up the phone, thought for a moment then He dialed Bro. Holmes number, ---waited a moment, --- Deacon Holmes, this is Pastor King. They talked for a moment about preacher and deacon things, then King came to the point of calling. "I want you to know that we are going to use your book, "the Brother Up Next." to lay the foundation for our district association. You are aware of course how people feel about you through out the state. Many church people do not like you, you are considered to be mean and stand off. You want to do your own thing. The problem is you are hard on people who work with you. But we have a place here with the association that fits your style. Brother you are one of a few people who can help us drag ourselves out of this mud and the mire. You can almost work alone, and the people that we will assign to your group, understand you. Not only do we want to get the association back to where it was, but we want it to be better than before. I am looking at a theme that was used by pastor F.J. of Dallas, Texas. It is a brilliant theme "Committed to Become a GREAT District Association. We commit to becoming a great District Association by:

(1) Keeping the Great Confession---Matthew 16:15-16. (90)

"He said unto them, But whom say ye that I am? And Simon Peter answered and said, Thou art the Christ, the S on of the Living God."

(2) Keeping The Great Commandment----Matthew 22:37-40.

"Jesus said unto them, Thou shalt love the Lord thy God with all thy heart, and with all thy soul, and with all thy mind. This is the first and great commandment. And the second is like unto it, thou shall love thy neighbor as thyself. On these two commandments hand all the Law and the prophets."

(3) Keeping the Great Commission.--Matthew 28:19-20. Mark 16:15-18.

"Go ye therefore, and teach all nations, baptizing them in the name of the Father, and of the Son, and of the Holy Ghost,: Teaching them to observe all things whatsoever I have commanded you: and, lo, I am with you always, even unto the end of the world." This will be how we will share with the public, what the convention is all about. We need to tell them in a few words that they can understand. It become our responsibility to teach them to practice what WE preach. We do that by the life we live in the trenches of Human Valley of Suffering. The life that is real, the pain that cause suffering, The disappointment that brings a man to sing the blues. The line of jealously that comes from the valley, that may cause a weak man to take his life. As you know that will require resources that we have never used before, both financial and committed people.

Rev. King stopped long enough to ask him if he had time to come over to Rev. Hinton's house. He informed him that sister Hinton was in the process of preparing the evening meal. He went on to tell him that they had been discussing the situation and needed his help. He asked them to give him an hour and he would be on their front porch. Rev. King laugh because he said, on the porch. None of the houses had porch's in that neighborhood. He was sharing with them what Holmes had said, when an ambulance with its red lights and siren pulled up next door, they looked out the window to see neighbors running toward the house. A few minutes after the ambulance arrived they heard a woman scream, they knew that it was the wife of the preacher next door. They turned from the window, running toward the door they knew something terrible had happen. and in no time they were inside the house trying to help in any way that they could. The attendant asked them to go into the other room, to give them space to work. The pastors shared with them who they were and that they were men of the cloth. They were asked to wait in the other room, and they would call them if they needed them. It was then that one attendant looked at the other and shook his head. Then they got on the phone. Finally they placed the blanket over the whole body, "The corner will be here soon."

Pastor you are too late, about all that you can do is comfort the family. I'm sorry, wish we could have done more, It was just too late, his heart failed him. The wife started to scream and beg. She asked the preachers if they could do something. The wife turned toward the two pastors, Can't you pray, you are suppose to know God personally. Tell God not to take him, no, not now.. She began to begging God not to take him now. She asked for a few days and he could take the both of them, but not now Lord, he is not ready. Lord please do not take him now, give us a little more time. Lord you know that he is not ready. If you are going to take him anyway, then let your mercy and your grace cover him all the way home. Then finally there were silence. When they bought the old man our of the house his whole body was covered. She mumbled to herself, the association killed him. They took from him everything that meant anything to him.--------now they took his life. The word says that you will reap what you sow.

Ray shook his head, then he spoke. "That old man was once a pastor, an office holder in the association. He was well thought of in his position of service. There was a time about twenty years ago, that the association was looking his way to be the moderator. He never gave up, he was always looking to be nominated for the position. As he got older and saw that they were never going to elect him moderator, he became more bitter by the year. His church was small and most of the members were senior people. They did not have the money to pay all the money that all three groups wanted for a leader in the association to pay. He once heard the moderator speak negative about him and that he was old foggy. He never forgave the association for what they done to their church. My understanding is when the church called them for an explanation, the office hung up on them. A month or so later they sent him a letter that he had been dropped from the association staff and was no longer needed.

He held an important office that he was proud off. But they cut him loose when they dismissed the church that he belonged to. He became so bitter that he stopped going to church.

The word has it that he had taken up drinking, there were nights that he would not let his wife back into the house until his daughter would come by cursing and waving her gun. Man, I want you to know that his daughter was mean, one night she hit him across the head with a coke bottle and almost killed him. After that he would not allow his daughter into his house. She would be standing at the gate cursing him with words that sailors didn't know. He would not say a word, just sat there in the window with his shot gun across his legs. His wife would be in the house crying, it was a sad situation.

Rev. King sat there with his head down. Then he asked who was their pastor. He was informed that their pastor lived out of town. He then inquired as to the name of the church. Again he was informed that they hardly went to church. Then he said that this will be the first church we will bring back into the fold. Old man Hinton could lead a hymn that would raise the hair on your head. He thought about their chairman of the board who lived in the neighborhood. He immediately called the chairman and informed him of what had happen. He asked him and his wife to meet them at the dead man's house. They were going to spend time in prayer and song, and bible reading. He then called the sister over the mission program who also lived with in a few blocks from the church.. He asked the ladies to think about "precious Lord take my hand" and "I need thee every hour". He and the old pastor would pray.

Rev. Hinton and Rev. King, with the women formed a circle around the recent widow. They prayed to God that he would grant her the power to survive in the absent of her husband. When they had finished praying, they looked toward Sister Hinton. She started out by saying, Now Lord, once more and again, your humble servant----) Sister Hinton talked to God as if he was holding her hand. She was the last to pray She would Rock from side To side and then she would throw her head back and say, "Well Lord, have mercy where mercy can be found.----Then she would shake her shoulders, drop her head backward, and then she would moan " (Down by the river I heard my master called and I said, yes Lord.) She caught her dress by the end of her garment, she held it tightly, shaking her head in tears, and when she ended her prayer she started to humming, "Pray For Me" They all joined in, and the house seem to be sweating from the ceiling and the windows that faced East.

Every once in a while old man Hinton's voice rose above the other voices. And you could hear, Yes Sir, Thank you Lord, Have Mercy Lord,. And before she closed the song, they all joined together, the old folks call this a "MOAN" it was different from a humming. People who had come to visit, gathered around them, and they would just humming, while the two pastors and their wives with the old preachers wife talked to the Lord on this occasion.

As they prepared to walk back to Rev. Hinton's house, they asked the new widow to spend the night with the Hinton's, until out of town family members had time to arrive. She agreed to go with them, then she stopped and looked at the rocking chair that he sat in, it was the only place he could find comfort. She walked over and toughed it, then she kissed her fingers and toughed the back of the chair. Then she turned and walked away. When they walked out of the house to return back to where they were, Rev. Hinton's house; there were still tears in their eyes. And you could still hear from one to another, "Thank Yea, Yes Lord, old lady Hinton got happy all over again, She kept saying, thank Yea, she kept repeating the same words. She caught her dress by the tail of her garment and began to a shuffle, turning round and round, they had to go and get her and carried her into the house. She was still saying Thank Ye. Lord. Bro. King was happy, he was humming with his arms wrapped around his body, yes Lord, Yes Lord, I hear yea Humming

The chairman of the deacon board and the missionary sister was getting out of their car. They spoke and shook hands before going in. Sister, King said to the group, we want to fill this room with the obedience of God. When they had song their last song, the old lady was smiling in tears. King said to the chairman of the board and missionary sister, This may not be the time to say this, if it is not forgive me, I mean this from the bottom of my heart. I want Rev. Hinton to meet with the deacons, sister hood, and preachers who are members of the church. There was a hesitation, we want you back in the district association. Sister we need new experience mature Christian lady to lead the Godly women of the district. I know you can do it, but you and your church will need to be a member of the D.A.. At this moment I welcome the Sweet Home Baptist Church is back in the D.A in good standings until after the meeting with Dr. Hinton.

Sister Hinton began to humming the song,

"I NEED THEE EVERY HOUR", She song that song so strongly until her body trembled. She folded her arms as she moved up from her seat. She moved up rocking her body side to side until she finally stood. She was holding her arms close to her body trembling in tears. Then finally she prayed. (The divine in her touched the divine in heaven and they agreed to her request) God was pleased, unconsciously they knew that this service was not their doing, and it was here that they accepted God's will for their lives. At the end of the service,

The diseased wife surprised them with a word of thanks and a warm handshake. She informed them that her husband would have given his life to be back into the D,A. He loved working with the men. He liked to be called bro. chairman, I would look at my husband and he was proud of the position that he held. She thanked Rev. King for putting some sun light into her life.

After the ambulance had left, the chairman Walker stood at the gate, steadying himself for support. He had never before witness or shared in a worship service that he had witness this night. His body, mind and soul was still on fire. He never knew that God could work such powerful, and eye opening cause of happening. He held onto the gate and dropped his head, "Lord,, I've never experienced anything like this in my life, if it is your will for me to live under the power of the Holy Spirit on this earth, here I am Lord use me." It was this feeling that woke up the front and back of his sleeping mind. As he stood there first looking back at the house that the dead man left, he looked down the streets, then in the direction of the four that disappeared into the house. wanted to become part of God working with those who care for the very best.

My God, he said to himself, I felt as if I were in a light whirlwind. I could feel myself being lifted up from where he was. I got caught up in this whirl wind and all I heard was this thundering sound of the Holy Spirit, letting me know that I had been accepted for something special. At the time I did not know what was going on; I just wanted to be a part of a glowing spirit that held me in suspense. From my mouth I uttered words that I did not understand. Words of bursting joy, the feeling of bursting wide open in the presence of God. My soul cried out a welcome message of acceptance.

Rev. King and Hinton was watching from behind the window as Walker stood leaning on the open gate. Finally King said, "This may be our man, if he is what a start for correction. The author Holmes pulled up and when he removed himself from his automobile, he recognized the deacon holding onto the gate looking at the gravel on the ground. Holmes got out of his car, walked over and spoke to the chairman, who was glad to see him. With total excitement he shared the death of the former deacon, the promise that King made and then the experience he had with worship. Holmes was about to walk away whenRev. King called out to the two men; He asked both men if they would come and have dinner with them. Both men looked at each other, together they walked toward the house. Suddenly deacon Walker stopped. "Does Rev. King have the authority to bring our church back into the district association?" Holmes smiled, put his arms around walker's shoulders, "Come and see.".

The meal was outstanding. It seem as if they were eating cautiously with reverence at each bite, It could be the worship service had not moved itself for what it had yet to do. The people in the room was not totally aware of what discussion would be next. They felt a strange power hovering over them, but no one said a word, they just quietly ate their meal. Finally sis.

Rev. King spoke up, " Dec. Walker. I understand you have eyes on sis. Spencer, she is a terrific young woman. She is known through the state and there is no rumor about her with any of the men, especially the preachers" They all smiled. Finally the deacon spoke up, we are just friends, very close friends. We have the kind of friendship that we rushes to each others aid if it was needed. I would give her my last, we support each other in every way." He fell silence for a moment, for the expression on his face told off on him. There were something there deeper than friendship, especially on the deacons part. Those around the table who was looking at him that this man loves this woman. Walked looked up at them and dropped his eyes toward his plate. "I don't know why we are discussing this; first I'm too old for her, I am 30 years her senior, my health issue's are from six months to six months; thirdly I don't have any money, just a house that is not paid for and a car I don't own, I am still working part time.

Sister Hinton said, "Deacon you seem to be trying to convince yourself that you are not for her. Why don't you let her make that decision. I can see that you love that woman. You should at least let her know how you feel. She may not be interesting in you, but it won't be for the three reasons that you gave. She could be waiting on you to move the friendship into a relationship. What if she wants to be your woman, you never know what's on a woman's mind. I've seen her take up for you many times in the past. She will not let anyone talk about you in her presence. You know as well as we, that there are many people that do not like you. They don't know why, they just don't like you. You don't make it any better, your knowledge of church administration and organization is far greater than the majority of the pastors in this state. I think it is only fair to her, she may feel the same way, or she just may need a man like you. At least give her a chance. You don't have to tell me, I know that you are afraid, you almost hope that she will say, that she likes it the way it is" Sis. Hinton had talked privately with some of the women in the district, they all agreed that his fear of something that they were not sure of, were keeping him from saying anything to her about how he felt. This was not the first time the two of them came up in church conversation.

Pastor King said, "The kind of time that the two of you will spend, if you are not married, there is going to be talk that will hurt the association. I,M not trying to force anything on you, matter of face on either of you; but I thank that this journey will need a man and wife. I have to agree that this is rushing things a little".

Sis. Hinton picked up the telephone book and looked up her number, she put her hand on the phone, then looked at bro. Walker.

"If she is interesting, would you ask her to be your woman. What I mean is, that she be your woman until there is a marriage. Walker I know that this woman want you, she just bloom when you walk into the room where she is." Rev. Hinton could not believe his ears. He looked at his wife as if he was finding all of this unbelievable. All the years that they had been married, he had never seen her is this role before. The look on her face cried out for him to say yes, as if she knew something that he did not know, or had heard and did not recognize or understand. Deacon I'll ask you again, if she will accept your invitation for her to be your woman, will you confess to her that you love her. With the understanding that she may not feel as you, and want to keep your relationship friendly. There was a long silence, then finally he said, "yes". Then he started mumbling something that no one could understand, it for sure was unintelligent, and made no sense to anyone including himself.

She picked up the phone, and when the phone was answered, she said, "Liz, this is sister Hinton." They chattered for a few minutes, then she said, "Deacon walker is here visiting with the pastors, we have finished out meal, sorry that we did not invite you. We are discussing church administration. As you know Rev. King have been asked to lead this group in hope that this association can get back on its feet. If you had the time, your input would be valuable. Would you come over and join us? Liz there is something else I want to talk to you about" Then she turned and went into the bedroom so that they could not hear her talk. She did not want to embarrass a scared Dec. Walker. "Sister Liz brother Walker have been liking you for a long time. You know that and I know that. You know that he is in love with you, there is no way that you can miss how he feels about you.

Do you have any interest at all in him past you'll friend ship?" There was a long pause, "I don't know if I understand what you are thinking or saying. I do not want to mess up the friendship that we have. We are very valuable to each other as we are." Liz I'm a woman and you are a woman, there are some things that women understand.

I do not believe that you don't know that Walker is in love with you. "He has said nothing to me about how he feels, he is always talking about how he appreciate the kind of friendship that we have.." liz, she cut her off, let me put it to you straight, is there any possibility that you would marry him if he asked you to be his wife." There were another long pause. "I will not say yes or no until we have had a time to talk about relationship or the possibility of getting married. Then Liz asked, "Why the hurry, what is going on" Liz I am your friend, do you like him past being a friend." Finally she said Yes, he is the kind of man that I have always wanted. He may not be the man, but he is like the man of my dreams, but marrying I am not saying that he is that man, just that he is like the man of my dreams."

Sister Hinton looked concerned, there were something about Liz voice that bothered her. Liz we were about to get into the structure of the district association. Why don't you come over and get in on the ground floor. There is not one important person that has ever been associated with this association that you don't know, or know how to contact the,." Twenty two and a half minutes Liz knocked on the door. She was smiling and looking cute. The girl was together and she knew it. She walked over to Dec. Walker, held out her arms, "What word have you been floating over here? He stood, smiled down on her and kissed her on the forehead. Gently she kissed him on the cheek and gave him a special smile. Dec. almost melted, he had never hugged her that way before. They had never kissed before, not even on the forehead. There were enough room for them to sit next to each other on the couch.

Rev. King looked at Liz and Walker, "Am I to understand that the two of you will be working together and the two of you want to know where the other stand. Walker looked at her, and she looked at him, they smiled and said "yes." Liz immediately got up from the couch, walked over to the window. Her eyes caught a cute little rabbit that seem to be looking back at her. What in the ---- is this rabbit doing out here? Her mind flipped back to two weeks ago on a late Friday evening on the steps of the court house. The husband that no body knew that she had, said his last good-by. "You can do whatever you want, but if you get married, I will kill the both of you and no questions asked". He walked away a few steps, turned and faced her "Your freedom may cost you your life. I am going to see what that church will do for you dead." He turned and walked away with some swagger. She took a deep breath, then noticed that the rabbit was facing up on her, and she could feel his eyes burning into her eyes. Then quicker than right now he was gone.

She felt a fear that caused her to tremble from the inside. Little beads of tears formed in the corner of her eyes. Out of the tear that fell from the left eye, she saw a raven, who looked at her strangely, then the tear fell to the floor and he was gone. She batted her eyes and looked toward the open space, she saw a buzzard sitting on a bare tree limb, he seemed to be looking back over his shoulders before he flew away. Then there were nothing, not even a cloud, not even a bird, just the wind limping alone to nowhere. She wondered, what in ---- does this mean. When she turned to face the group, they looked different to her, they seem not to be paying her any attention.

That is except Sis. Hinton, she almost looked like a rabbit about the face, then she dropped her eyes and all was normal. She came back to where D ec. Walker was sitting. He looked at her strangely. Finally she began to hear Rev. King talking " sister Liz we will ask you to be the secretary for this group, or committee. There will be others added to this committee. You will be the general secretary for the whole group. When I want to know something I will come to you. There will be seven of us at first, then that group will be extended to twelve. The twelve group, will do most of the traveling. The first seven of us will work in the Metro-plex, close in to the heart of the city. But all of us is subject to call whenever we are needed. Rev. King explained to them what the state has shared with him, about what they wanted from his leadership. They wanted the Texas district association back on its feet, so that the area would be proud of her.

Rev. King looked at Dec. Walker and then at Sis Liz, " Sister

Liz if you are waiting for Dec. Walker to ask you to marry him, it will never happen. I agree with sis. Hinton, this man love you, but he is afraid. On the other hand no one know how you feel. Sis. Don't get into anything before its time. This association will survive without the two of you getting married. However, I must say that the building of this structure can be more effective with the two of you together; putting your heads together in late night session before day. Liz, spoke up, Wait, wait, we don't have to get married to make this association effective". Then she put her arms around him. "this is my friend, I am going to look after him and take care of him as long as I have the strength.

Why don't the two of you get married right now, at this moment. I keep marriage license in my bag. Those words brought a fear to Liz that caused her to tremble. "NO, NO,,O, SHE SAID, I will take care of him, but not to marry him. That is out of the question". Then she dropped her head without looking at Dec. Walker. Then she raised her head and spoke softly. "Rev. King if you get in touch with God and he promises me safety until I have accomplished his will on this earth., I will marry De. Walker".

She said these words out of the middle of nowhere. Everyone was taken back, they did not know what to say. Then she held Walker's hand, she looked at Rev. King. "If you will contact God right now and he guarantee you that I will be safe, I will marry this brother. Finally Liz smiled. Rev. King did not smile because he felt her desire for assurance of her safety.

He was trying to fix it in his mind how this was to be done, when God spoke to him underneath the silence of his mind. "Tell her not to fear man for I am greater that man, I can even change minds for those who believe." When King repeated to Liz what God had said, they had to catch her, she started to shout, throw her arms, tears and mucus went every where, She was shouting, thank you Lord, Yes Lord, have mercy Lord, she just started to go round and round, thank you Lord. When she was out of breath, they helped her to her seat.

Finally she said "I'm brave" Then she reached out and caught him by the hand. They held hands and looked each other in the eyes. There were something that troubled Walker. He stood and walked to the window where Liz had just left. Looking out at the thin air that was going no where. Wind that is so valuable that life cannot exist without its presence. Liz walked over to where he was standing, "What is wrong, I thought that you would be happy. I've known for a long time how you felt about me. Now here we are, neither of us can run for there is no where to run." Walker turned toward her, then toward all of them. "I have prostrate cancer. I have had it for over ten years. Matter of fact I did not know that I would live this long. God is walking with me daily, it is a daily walk with him that keep me on top of the earth. I take one shot every six months, I never know when they will tell me that the shot can't do me any good." He turned toward Liz, "Liz I love you more than life itself. I love you so much, I cannot stand to see you make this kind of mistake." She walked into his arms with a big smile on her face. "If I can have the best of you for six months, or a year, or however many years that God gives you, I want them for myself. I feel as if I'm a blessed woman. There is nothing that can happen to me as wonderful as you." She caught him by the hand and they walked to the couch and sat down. "don't rob me of you for as long as you can love me as if there is no tomorrow. I know about your cancer, there is nothing that we cannot work out, nothing."

Walker turned toward Rev. King, I'm so scared that I can hardly talk. They all laughed "What are we waiting for, you are robbing me of some of the time I have left." Then they smiled and the wedding, better yet, the marriage took place out of love and need.

Rev. King pulled out yellow secretary pads and pencils. What is the written foundation that we are going to build the association on.

It must be evangelism and healing for damaged emotions." Liz held up her hand. "Let us pull together a team of men and women for the soul purpose of closing that back door. We will teach every church in the district association how to close the back door. But in the meantime, we will have to practice the art ourselves. and keeping them connected to God's word." Liz, went on to say that she had studied a book sometime ago. It was called closing the back door, It was written by, Alan F. Harre, in his book he had this this to say, "The lack of personal contact is seen by some inactive as the reason why people drop out initially and do not return subsequently to active parish participation. These responses seem to confirm Womack's contention that a congregation cannot grow any larger than it has the ability to care for a specific number of people. He contends that there is a direct relationship between a church's base of operation efficiency and effectiveness and its members size."

Rev. Hinton, "One of the things that we have overlooked in the convention and the district association: We must help people realize how important it is to know what it is that God want them to do. No, No I don't mean that we should talk about what we ought to de, we must lead this association in ministries and work shop to drive home the importance of God's word upon believers." Sister King, "We should set up a crack team of men and women, maybe three who are experts on steward ship. Who have a compassion for the welfare of the membership" Another person knew what they wanted to say was not part of the foundation, but leaders needed to meet every three months. It is important to catch things before conflict set in, so that we can keep the ship upright.

Rev. King held his hands up. "Hold on, let us not move too quickly. Lets go back to the beginning. We are in this position primary because of the disobedience of leadership toward God's word. We have made excuses and gave cock-eyed reasons for not obeying the word of God. But most of all we lied to God to his face and allowed our love to crumble into small pieces. For the last twelve or eighteen years our function have not been to help the membership. The love we once had is like a vapor that moves without direction. It eats up space and time, but have only enough substance to kill the soul. Power, greed and compliancy have spoiled the white shirt that Christians once wore. If we don't go back to the basis, our ways and action will usher in the wrath and anger of God."

He went on to say that the next matter that have to be faced, is the organizational structure. He looked toward Liz. He wanted her to study the organizational charts on the internet, find the one that best benefit's the organization. The two of them will be working with Dec. Holmes in this matter. She was to draw up a thirty two block chart. They would fill them in as they go. All of the blocks would not be filled in with either persons or ministry. But the purpose of the blocks will give a direction as to where the association is going. He had decided not to wait until all the people were accounted for, but to put the chart together as soon as possible. He wanted this information handy, so that when people who have a need to know would ask, he would have something to show them. Because the structure would be different than before; it would be important for people in the know to look and observe how the set up would affect them and their church. He informed Liz that she would not be in charge of that committee, but her insight is important to him, because she would reporting directly to him.

Once the organizational chart have been set in motion, a small church in Dallas has a brother who has an extensive knowledge of church charts. I know him well. He will not stop until it is finished and the information on the chart will be one of the best. Liz I am going to get you his telephone number. Have him to go by Providence Baptist Church on 67 in Dallas, Texas. I know that pastor from our time in seminary, I will give him a call and I will call this brother, Mark and let him know that you will be making contact with him. You don't have to worry about him making eyes at you, he is strictly business. Holmes Will be the person over the evangelistic ministry. I also want him to be a part of closing the back door." He hesitated for a moment, : Helping churches to keep the people that they have, is a problem that we must solve. This is his field and his love. He will not talk evangelism, he is evangelism, from morning to midnight. He is the person who will make this organization effective. His strength is the org. chart, evangelism, closing the back door and spiritual gifts. He is tough, but don't let him scare you, he knows what he is doing.

Rev. King sat back in his chair. He wanted them to slow down, he could see that they were moving in a hurry.

He warned them that every important org. in Christianity, evangelism is at the foundation of every group. But yet a few months down the road it limps to the wayside. It will not happen here. He informed them that he will see that it does not happen here. Then he went on to say evangelism should be an effort to see controlling principals governing the movement of the master in the hope that our own labors might be conformed to a similar pattern. We all ought to know the principals underlying our ministry. Principals which determines our methods. If you choose, you could call this attitude Jesus strategy of evangelism. He hesitated for a moment.--No brother, sister or leader should attempt his or her responsibility without accepting the ability to lead to lead an unsaved person to Christ. Evangelism is more than leading the unsaved to Christ; it is also an attitude and mindset to please God at any cost.

The evangelistic build up of the association must be tied to the city wide and the local church. At some point we must realize that it is time for the church to realistically face the situation. Our days of trifling are running out. The great commission thrust of the gospel into new frontier has largely lost its power. The church has failed at the responsibility of building men for the mission. Maybe it is because it requires constant personal attention, much like the father gives his children. There is a lot of talk in the church about evangelism and Christian nurture, but little concern for personal association when it becomes evident that such work involves the sacrifice of personal indulgence.

Many of today churches are teaching witness as you go. The problem with that is few people will share the gospel with the lost. They will ask people to come to church and have a good time. They will leave the core of the responsibility hanging out there and unsaved people not given a change to accept Christ or reject him. One cannot share the gospel if they have not received Christ as their savior and Lord. One cannot share the gospel if they have unrepented sin in their life. They cannot share the word of God if they are in a state of backsliding.

Holmes had been quiet all evening. Sitting there as if he was in deep thought. Finally he spoke, "In the district association we need to lead the way for our local churches. There is an area that we fear to some point, but its need is paramount. God spoke of it all through the new testament. He gave instructions to his disciples and he did not leave this ministry without instructions. I feel as if this may be the only black district association in this country, who has a deliverance ministry. With the churches falling away from the faith, doing what they want to do and still get to heaven. This is the time where the D.A. step up and be accounted for. The fear that we have of demons cast some doubts about our willing to try and do what God has instructed us to do.

> Let us look at two or three scriptures: And these signs shall follow them that believe: IN MY NAME shall they cast out devils. (Mark 16:17)

> But ye shall receive power, after that the Holy Ghost is come upon you. (Acts 1:8)

> Then he called his twelve disciples together, and gave them POWER AND AUTHORITY OVER ALL DEVILS, AND TO CURE DISEASE (Luke 9:1)

And the seventy returned again with joy, saying, Lord even the devils are subject unto us through thy name. And he said unto them, I beheld Satan as lightening fall from heaven. Behold, I give unto you power to tread on serpents and scorpions, and over all the power of the enemy; and nothing shall by no means hurt you. (Luke 10:17-19).

The process of expelling demons is called deliverance. Deliverance is not a panacea--a cure all. Yet it is an important part of what God is doing in relationships to the current revival in the church. Some expect too much from deliverance and others expect too little. We honestly need to find out what part of deliverance can play in in each of our own lives and receive whatever benefit it offers. But in the meantime Demons are spiritual enemies and it is the responsibility of each Christian to deal with them directly in spiritual warfare.

Jesus established the pattern of team work for His disciples. When he sent the twelve out in ministry he sent them out two by two. When he commissioned the seventy he also sent them out two by two.

Other ministry teams are found in the book of acts. On the first missionary journey there were Paul, Barnabas and John Mark. Later there were Paul and Silas. Team ministry is a principal of scripture. It is especially suitable and effective in deliverance ministry.

Liz sat there for a few moments not saying a word.. It was not just because she was quiet, but it was the look of disappointment on her face. She looked at Rev. King in a curious way, she thought to say something, then changed her mind. By now everyone was looking at her, and she soon made up her mind to speak. "Before many of you knew me I was married to a man who could not kick the habit. I loved him deeply, so much so I felt as if I could not do without him. He told me the night before the wedding, that he had a habit he could not kick. He told me that he loved me, and with me in his life he could kick anything. I did not know what to do or think, so I married him. Our marriage lasted until his death, over an overdose of drugs. I was the most miserable woman in the world. I tried his drugs to make him happy, only the good Lord kept me in my right mind. Our children suffered greatly and they are suffering now. They blame their malfunction on me for marrying him. And some time I get caught up in my own self pity.

She hesitated for a moment and folded her arms; she was trying not to tear up before grown people. She said to them we have got to find a way to save these little children in the drug infested and moral corrupt environment of which they are raised. They cannot take themselves out of the family structure where they have been brought up. We must give them protection and preserve their souls while they are trying to learn to be capable young and women in our society.

She went on to ask the body if the deliverance ministry could cover the mental attitude of drug malfunction. She said that her biggest concern is little children who get so caught up on drugs until they cannot study and learn at school. She went on to say that she knew people who would assist the district in sending three or four people to a special school to learn the secret of the trade. Here they can learn and practice the techniques for keeping children from getting mixed up with drugs. She said that any help that they can develop, us it with the kids in mind. You can't help all children, but you must recognize the one's that can be helped. Even with this recognition there will be some failures. She believes that when society see the convention putting their best foot forward; they would receive resources of personnel and money.

When they had finished discussing the concern of Liz; Rev. King spoke. It is going to be hard getting the children out of the drug culture. We can start helping the children by helping their parents. Especially the parents who are looking for a way out of an environment; that have trapped them beyond their ability to escape. There are those who are struggling, but without help they keep falling back into a deeper pit of despair.

We believe that drugs is demonic inspired; it is Satan's way of destroying generation after generation. I agree with sister Liz, this is another area that we will have to tackle. We need to give new born babies a chance to survive. They did not ask to come here, we bought them here let us see if we can do a better job helping they to become every day adults.

No local church will be forced to start a deliverance ministry. Where there is fear, the local pastors will be asked to take their time, and give his people time to learn. Faith is Jesus Christ and believing in his word is required for success. Time will be given in the restored Baptist Training Union to teach the concept of deliverance. This session of study and practical advancement into the depth of God's will, has to be done correctly. Much study will be required for this ministry to function as God intended. Fear and doubt are the greatest enemies of a sincere believer. But the time will come when Satan will try to embarrass God in his own house. When Satan confronts believers on Sunday morning with tactics that is unbelievable. Voice changing to that of a hiss, sometime a growl, and at other time with a high pitch that is almost deafening, turn into snakes that crawl around inside God's house, when their heads will turn around on their shoulders: people will run over each other because of fear. Others will stand around, in doubt, and not knowing what to do. God has warned us many times to be prepared for the coming of the power of Satan. The fact is he has always been here on planet earth, but the weakness in the morality of the church will give him authority to control lives that once belong to God. The word of God enforces who Satan is; GOD ALL MIGHTY AND HE NEVER FAILS OR CAN BE OVERCOME BY ANY POWER.

We will further discuss this issue further when the whole transforming committee has been assembled. Until we do, make sure that you keep our plans off the streets. Misunderstanding will kill any plan, regardless of how good it is. We want to help people, but fear can hinder the progress of the best laid plan, even those who have been proven to be successful. There is nothing above the word of God, but fear can keep it from being effective. Let us look at one more issue The core committee of men and women will consist of seven people. They will make the plans to share with the body of leaders in the association. Yes we will make changes, but we will not change every thing. People of the church does not like change, we can never forget that; but if you tell them how the change involves around them and for them, and if the leader has confidence of the people, his plan will work.

The teaching of the association is that the first year, do nothing about change except help the church to run smoothly. If the deacons come to a pastor and share the need for change in a certain place, respond to it quickly. In the second year, make a few minor changes with the consent of leadership. If you cannot convince them about the change, put it back for another day. If God have given it to you, it must eventually come forward. But at a later day, with different circumstances. On the third year after all have studied the organizational chart, they will see where you are going, and most of them will be behind the pastor. In the fifty year, you will be ready to put forth the(full whole) plan that God has given you. Make sure that the pastors and deacons understand the concept of change.(Only God will give the (vision) to the pastor, but it will be confirmed in spiritual deacons when the pastor bring it forward. The spirit of the two groups will agree. The vision will be brought to the deacons and trustees and when they have worked out what God had intended for the church, and the welfare of the congregation, they will present the vision as a plan of the church. When the church have shared, and become excited about the plan; it become the goal of the church to be obedient to the spirit of God.

The vision, plan and goal is under the guidance of all mighty God. The church in relation to the direction of God has its other work cut out to help reach the goal that has been set before them. The Brother Up Next, has proven to be a road map to the church, as they are working toward their goal. Let us set down a few things that the church must constantly go through. They must become perfect in the knowledge that God has given them as believers. We must remember that not only are we commander to save souls; We care instructed to make disciples out of those you win to Christ, and make disciple makers out of disciples. The church must always be on the look out for young men, teaching and instruction in the way of the Lord. If one desires to be a deacon or a preacher, give him all the support that you can. Good preachers and good deacons are hard to find.

In the western part of Texas, small country towns are without qualified men to serve as pastors or deacons.

They must go to the next largest town to find people who say they are preachers. What they usually find are men who are looking for the money and power as pastor. In many cases, some of these preachers are not even saved. No young men are on trial for a deacon, and in some cases there are no deacons in the entire church. Women and out of town preachers are carrying on. There are many small towns who have not had a young man called into the ministry for fifteen year. They had not made a deacon in a longer time than that. Some pastor have turned to women deacons. Brothers this is never good, it is against the word of God. It doesn't matter how hard it is to train men, it is worth the effort. The association has a lot of work to do, too much in a short period of time. Let us look quickly at some subjects that the association will teach, believe, and practice; because they will become of the heart of the church and soul of the association.

Remember these studies are found in the three books that we will be studying from. The Bible, Brother up Next and Doctrine and Administration of the church. All twelve people in this committee group will know its teaching more than anything that you know.

Let us look at the contents of the brother up next.

In-Active Drop-Ours.

It is a form of closing the back door. The rite of passage by which people become members of religious communities are well known. The rite of passage by which people leave the "Tipping phenomenon' remain unexplored.

Stewardship, budging, success and financial responsibility, Success is knowing your purpose in life, growing to reach your maximum potential, and sowing seed that benefit others.

Spiritual gifts.

It is unfair to the church to allow a believer to operate as a leader without knowing his or her spiritual gift.

Evangelism.

One cannot transform a world except as individuals in the world are transformed, and the individuals cannot be changed except as they are molded in the hands of the master.

Small Group Ministry's

Church growth studies have found that for a church to assimilate new people effectively it must have an average of seven small groups for each one hundred adult members.

Mother and Father Board.

Pure religion and undefiled before God and the father is this, to visit the fatherless and widows in their affliction, and to keep himself unspotted from the world.

Attitude For Belonging

You are the only person who can do anything about your attitude.

Respect For God. But your iniquities have separated you from your God; your sins have hidden His face from you, so that he will not hear.

Obedience/Commitment.

Without obedience to God and a commitment to his word, there is no relationship.

Discipline Restored.

When the church fails to render discipline as God commanded, the sin of disobedience rest upon the congregation.

Power of Love.

A new commandment I give you; Love one another. As I have

loved you, so you must love one another. By this all men will know that you are my disciple, If you love one another.

Effective Leadership.
To build trust, a leader must exemplify competence, connection, and character.

Power of Discipleship.
After Blind Barimaeus had received his sight, he did not selfishly go on his way when his need was met. He began with need, went on to gratitude, and finished with loyalty-and that is a perfect summary of the stages of discipleship.

Conflict Resolution.
We must understand that some conflict are simply minor nuisances that we accept as natural components of existence. Others keep our relationships from realizing their full potential, and some become so severe that they do irreparable damage to individuals, families, work places, and entire communities.

These will be ministries that the district will learn well, then go to the local churches and teach them. This is especially true with those churches that was dropped off the list. The deliverance ministry will remain with the association. We will not try to organize a group of churches to function in this area. Too many mistakes can happen when people are untrained, or go out on their own. The district will control this ministry. The other ministry they will control is Conflict Resolution. Conflict resolution is a little complex, a little difficult to understand. However, they will be available on call on any of the local churches that have a need.

Deacon Holmes was looking down, but there were concern on his face. Apparently something had been left out. As he sat there all the others was looking at him. They wondered what off the wall kind of question was he going to ask. Then he straighten up, pecked on the table a few times, then stopped.. "You brought Beth Eden back into the association is that the end of the process. You say that they can come back, and if they want to, they are back. Is there a process that will drive their return, a commitment that the church and the association knows about."

Rev. King got up from his seat, walked over to the window that Bro. Walker was looking out. He looked at the house where they had earlier taken the man of the house, to the morgue.

A man who died a bitter, disappointed man, driven by an attitude called hate. A man who lived without a good night sleep for a mighty long time. A man who thought about death, then convinced himself that there were no life after death. There were no such thing as heaven and hell. He had gone so far as to think there were, and there is no God, who had a son who died on an old rugged cross for our sins. And when he became sin for us, his father could not look upon his son for three hours. Finally he said that into thy hands I command thy spirit. It was a sad time, and yet a time for a new beginning.

Rev. King turned and faced the group, "There is one other thing that I want to run by you. I want to see how you feel while our group is small, while you do not have time to think about the negatives. And yet do not make a hasty decision, it is far too important a step in the rebuilding of this district association. Don't misunderstand me, we will discuss this issue later. We will call in some of the local pastors that we trust their spiritual life. I am thinking about developing a think tank made up of mostly women. Hand picked, because of their dedication to the word of God. They will be single and married, but none of then can be presently living in sin. Their qualifications will be strict, as the woman who lost her husband and filled the rest of her days praying in the temple daily.

Rev. King could tell that the group were ready to go home, but there were something that he must let then try it on for size. He wanted them at take time to think the process through. Although he had convinced himself that he was going to perform the rite.

He had decided that regardless to what anyone said, he was going through with it. If he went through with the project and it did not work, people would laugh at him and call him a fool. They will say that he should have known better than try something as stupid as that. He thought for a moment; his wife would leave him and take the children; or maybe she would take their shot-gun and blow his brains out. Failure, no failure could not be a thought after God has put his stamp on the expectations of the future; a time which begins now and change lives for the eternal kingdom.

CHAPTER #9

Reverse marriage

"He that hath my commandments, and keepeth them, he it is that loveth me: and he that loveth me shall be loved of my father, and I will love him." (John 14:21)

He could tell by the look on the faces of those sitting in Rev. Hinton's house, that they were getting tired, but the hook had not been set yet. He knew that this was the time, if he let it pass, he may never get the opportunity again. He knew that the project that he was to introduce, had to be close to earth shattering. He thought about the process of (reversal marriage.) We have an issue that we must face that is a little out of the ordinary, but we must face it now. This will give you time to think of its contents before we meet together in a few weeks.

(The process is called, A Reverse Marriage). A process where the churches who had been dismissed from the association would be re-joined in a marriage ceremony of re-commitment. They would re-dedicate themselves to the Cap/Rock District Association. But this time every person that is involved, has taken another look at Jesus Christ, they have committed themselves to the obedience of an all mighty God. It is a ceremony occupied by a covenant agreement between the church, the association, and God. The local church where it is to be held and the association will agree on the date and time of this event. The service will be in the hands of the Cap/Rock District Association. The moderator will be in charge and each church will have a program as to what is said and done. The national brotherhood union will be invited, but will not participate. Because this is a new piece of information, and because of the size of the church there will be a somewhat limited expectation of the locals who would like to attend. Every effort will be made to have this event at the church on Ferguson Rd, where CD'S and DVD'S can be made during the ceremony.

Let me first of all go through some of the things that will happen on this special occasion. Mind you this is not complete, there is much work to be done. I will walk through the exercise as if we were actually going through the graduation or marriage.

Thirty minutes before the session began, all windows and doors will be closed and locked, except the main door into the sanctuary. Remind you, the churches involved will be saturated with this information. They will be informed of every minute of this event. Especially the locking of the doors. Even though the doors are locked, there will be people on the doors, in case we have an emergency. We want to make sure that all fire codes are followed and escape routes are open if needed. No one would be allowed into the sanctuary until after the deliverance team have agreed with God on the cleansing of the sanctuary.

Before anyone enters the Sanctuary the deliverance team will bind all demons spirits in the room. The reason for this is, when bound they cannot interfere with the service. When the team have completed their chore, angels will be positioned at each window and each door. All seats will remain open until the churches involved has taken their seat. It may be that only churches involved will have a place to set. In that case they will be asked to the fellowship hall where screens has been set up for that purpose.

Let us assume that the building will be full and the locals will be in the fellowship hall. At ten minutes of the hour, music will be played powerfully and softly with a human message. One church at a time will march in with the pastor leading his congregation, followed by the deacons, associate preachers if there are any, and then the congregation. After the last one have turned into their seats, another church will come in and take their seats, until all churches have been seated.

The deliverance team that have cleansed the sanctuary of all spirit's that is not like Jesus Christ. They will move at a place that is not connected to the service, but are prepared to response if needed. When the signal is given to began the service. All preachers and deacons who are not involved in the service will sit in the choir stand. The pastors who are involved will sit in the chairs behind the rostrum. The moderator will sit directly behind the pulpit. The musicians will take their place, the ushers would have already placed themselves for service. The moderator will stand and call for the deacons to involve song and prayer. They will sing old hymns and read scripture of repentance. When the song and prayer has ended; the moderator will stand and pray a short prayer for God to accept this service. That his will be done, nothing but his will is to be receive.

The pastor or pastors of the churches will stand. Soft music will be playing when no spoken word is sounding. Each pastor of the churches standing will say. " We are here, We are ready, We are prepared and We are committed.

The devotion will be done by deacons from established churches in the association. Deacons who will come in together immediately after the room have been cleansed. They will take their seats across the front row. All across the building The entire church or churches will march in after the devotion. The pastor of the church where the event is being held, will stand, We welcome you to the house that God has chosen for this purpose "We are ready, we are prepared and we are able, and we are committed. Thank God for your presence" Then he will sit down.

The moderator of the Cap/Rock District Association, will step forward; behind him will be seated all of the officer of the association, who are men and preachers. Non-preacher members will be seated in the choir stand. The moderator will take his bible, open it to (Jude chapter #1 verse 18-25. NIV).

"They said to you, in the last times there will be scoffers who will follow their own ungodly desires. These are the men who divide you, who follow mere natural instincts and do not have the Holy Spirit.

But you, dear friends, build yourself up in your most Holy Faith and Pray in the Holy Spirit. Keep yourselves in God's love as you wait for the mercy of our Lord Jesus Christ to bring you eternal life.

Be merciful to those who doubt, snatch others from the fire and save them; to others show mercy, mixed with fear--hating even the clothing stained by corrupt flesh.

To him who is able to keep you from falling and to present you before his glorious presence without fault and with great joy--to the only God our savior be glory, majesty, power and authority, through Jesus Christ our Lord, before all ages, now and forevermore! Amen."

The moderator then asks the pastors, preachers and deacons of the churches involved to stand. Then he says carefully, "These are the men that you have chosen to lead you. They are the one you believe God has called inspired to be your leader, to sit in your sick room, share the gospel when the time is called upon, to marry your sons and daughters, to bury your dead, to share with you about your careers and pray to God on your behalf and to stand in in your stead when grief has overcome you. These are the men that you trust your financial resources with. When he gets weak you rise to the occasion on his behalf. At the end of the day, you are ready to rest and God have found your activity pleasing to He and the father."

"Brothers," He slowly looks over the audience with a solemn look on his face. Then he began to speak slowly but not dragging. "there are no single attribute in the life of a man who desires to be pastor, preacher or deacon which is more important than LEADERSHIP. Leadership skills car be learned, but leadership that causes people to follow the individual have been with him since birth. People show leadership skills before they have been asked to serve on any committee or ministry. They must show the ability to make good sound decisions and solid judgment. They must be able to work through difficult times in pressure situations. You, the man must be able to keep standing even though you are knocked down. He may not be aware of it himself, bit other people see leadership ability in your every day activity."

"Brothers you may be seated. I have talked with the leadership extensively of all the churches involved; and each one of you are committed to each other. The growth of the individual, of the church, of the district association and the state general convention. But most of all to God all mighty. Your pastor have talked to you and answered questions, until what we are doing has been made clear to you. If there is a question that you still do not understand about your church being a part of the district association, briefly make it clear now" He hesitates for a moment, looking over the group. Then quickly he says, thank you. "From this point on, this service will be about the pastors, preachers and deacons. we want you to listen carefully, if there are any disagreements from what you thought and what he is saying, write it down on a piece of paper, and in a minute we will address it.

The moderator would then ask each pastor, who are committee to this D.A. what is the evidence of his calling to preach and then to pastor. Only when a pastor goes astray of the word of God will the moderator ask for some clarification as to why he thinks that way. The district association is under the umbrella of OLD SCHOOL teaching. The pastor and preachers are asked to bring their pastor guide and deacons with them. This is followed by

the preachers who are associated with the church. A strong sharing of what the reason for issuing a preaching license and his ordination by his local church. The preachers will not be questioned, but the instruction to them will be stern. When trouble rise the preachers and the pastors can move on, but the deacons belong to and with the church. Their instructions are a little different; if the preacher or pastor leave, the deacon's responsibility is to carry on the church. Even to the point of bringing a Sunday morning message in the absent of a preacher. It is their responsibility to see to it that the pulpit is occupied each Sunday morning.

The deacons will not allow another denomination preacher in the pulpit. When they bring a preacher to preach; they will be sure that he does not preach a different doctrine than they believe. When the church is without a pastor, the district association does not take over; but they step in and assist the church in all ways to help them stay together, and find a replacement. The D.A. will set down with the deacons and trustees; they will come to an agreement of moving the church forward. The D.A. Will step aside, and stand ready to help the church in any way that they can. Remember, the association, it is not their job to run the church, but to assist it alone the way.

The Moderator stood there for a while first looking at the membership who are accepting themselves back into the district association. He turned and looked at the pastors sitting in their places. Then he turned to the deacons and asked them to come down front and face the audience. He asked the congregation if they would spare him a little time. The deacons came down and faced the audience. The moderator lifted his bible so that he could read from the Holy word. He chose (1 Tim. 3:1-10 NIV) "Brothers will you agree to keep this covenant that God has shared with you, for the keeping of your soul, and to cover the responsibility that lie ahead of you.?" They all bowed their heads Yes. He asked the pastors of each church to stand and face the deacons from the audience. This is to the both of you, a commitment that when broken is a sin and must be repented to God, for only he can forgive you. Listen carefully"
" Here is a trustworthy saying; If anyone sets his heart on being an overseer, he desires a noble task. Now the overseer must be above reproach, the husband of but one wife, temperate, self-controlled, respectable, hospitable, able to teach, not given to drunkenness, not violent but gentle, not quarrelsome, not a lover of money. He must

manage his own house family well and see that his children obey him with proper respect.(If anyone does not know how to manage his own family, how can he take care of God's house.

He must not be a recent convert, or he may become conceited and fall under the same judgment as the devil. He must also have a good reputation with outsiders, so that he will not fall into disgrace and into the devils trap.

Deacons, likewise are to be men worthy of respect, sincere, not indulging in much wine. And not pursuing dishonest gain. They must keep hold of the deep truths of the faith with a clear conscious. They must first be tested; and then if there is nothing against him, let them serve as deacons." The moderator will ask the wives to stand and join their husbands.

"In the same way, their wives are to be women worthy of respect, not malicious talkers but temperate and trustworthy in everything."

"A deacon must be the husband of but one wife and must manage his children and his household well. Those who have served well gain an excellent standing and great assurance in their faith in Jesus Christ."

The moderator closed his Bible. He asked the pastors to sit down, and he asked the deacons to face him. "I know that all of you, that is each of you that stand before me, do not understand the seriousness of the oath that you are taking. I am asking the pastors to set under the teaching of the D.A. concerning this covenant that we call an oath. Brothers, the D.A. want you to committee yourself to this word of God. A commitment sets in your heart that you know what God want you to do, the attitude of a believer, and the mindset of a true follower of Christ. I want you to commit your life, your intentions and your desires to being obedient to this, God's word. You are to talk this word, teach it quarterly in your men ministry meetings. You are to warn a brother when he seem to be moving off the mark Then he looked at his bible, almost as if he was weighting to get good balance.

He turned to Ezekiel 33:12-16niv. "Therefore, son of man, say to your countrymen, The righteousness of the righteous man will not save him when he disobeys, and the wickedness of the wicked man will not cause him to fall when he turns from it. The righteous man, if he sins, will not be allowed to live because of his former righteousness. If I tell the righteous man that he will surely live, but then he trust righteousness and does evil, none of the righteous things he has done will be remembered; he will die for the evil he has done. And if I say to the wicked man, you will surely die,, but he then turns away from his sin and does what is just and right---if he gives back what he took in pledge for a loan, return what he has stolen, follow the decree that give life, and does no evil, he will surely live: he will not die. None of the sins he has committed will be remembered against him. He has done what is just and right, he will surely live."

Then he closed his bible, he seemed to be a little nervous, but his eyes was always study. Brothers, do not get angry when a brother pull your coat tail, even if he is over zealous. I want you to bow your head, close your eyes and in silence promise God that you will be obedient to this, thy word for the keeping of thy soul. Thank you, you may be seated.

Pastors you are being unfaithful to God when you do not teach your deacons to be obedient to the qualifications that God's word has set before us. It is your responsibility to know and teach your leaders how to be obedient to God's word. The deacons inability to function as Christian leaders, to be keepers of God's word, to live a life pleasing to God under the commitment of God's command, rest with the pastor. If a deacon refuses to be a deacon according to what God want him to be, this is God's church, remove him! There is no place for intentionally sinning deacons, I am not saying that they will never sin, but they must not be sinning deacons in the eye of God. Disobeying God never misses the watchful eye of God. It is not something that he cast into the sea of forgetfulness. When you do a brother or sister wrong and hurt the heel of their soul, you must pat dearly. Brothers, if you don't want to be a deacon as God has intended for you to do, you may now move yourselves from the rank of deacon of this association. The church where you worship will handle this conflict at home. But you cannot be a deacon in this association without full commitment. This association is built on men.

An old man who could barely walk, placed his cane in its place and he looked back at the moderator; on his way to his seat. He was trembling a little. The moderator acknowledge his tenure with a lot of years, and then he turned around and looked at his people. He kind of looked down and with a strong trembling voice "I love the Lord, He heard my cry and pitted every groan." Then the church picked it up and the house rocked with wavering heads. When he completed his song, another old deacon began to pray, he talked to God as if God was in reach of his soul. He begged God to help them be the church that would honor Him, one that is preparing for its home going in heaven. As soon as he closed his prayer, a young man not yet forty years old, "Guide me over thy great Jehovah", then he called out to the church to help him, and the roof wanted to come off the house.

When the deacons sat down, The moderator looked at the pulpit, he put his arms around it and they rocked for a moment then he leaned backward with his arms gripping the pulpit, he broke off on "Pray for Me". The organist quickly caught on and began to make the instrument talk a natural tune. The moderator trembling voice was good for effect. Tears was falling from eyes all over the building, shouting burst out all down the isle, white hand chief was wavering, and people saying yes Lord,

Yes Lord, oh God all mighty., help me Lord. When the worship event had ended, he took a white handkerchief from his pocket and cried like a baby. Finally he gathered his composure, looked toward the door, smiled a little and shook his head. If I could live the rest of my life in this spiritual human valley of suffering, feeling the tough of God always in my presence. Then he shook his head.

"Brothers, I am going to read to you the Brotherhood Motto, if you will agree with the keeping of the motto, say yes and raise your right hand before you say yes or no, I want you to know that as a brotherhood, you are not a keeper of what you are about. You sound good, and there are smiles all over the room. Brothers you don't live what you say that you are. You give evangelism as the foundation for who you are, but somewhere you have forgotten who Jesus Christ is, because there are but a few being saved in this city. Now brothers, don't say anything, just listen closely. The angels of God is sitting beside you, listening to your response and your dedication. 'Teach the word in the home, with a consecrated heart, following in the foot step of the savior,, leading all men to God." Then he looked up at them, they all agreed.

The definition of brotherhood; The brotherhood is a group of Consecrated Christian Men undergoing all the programs of the Church and the denomination.' ok

The Origin of the brotherhood; The Biblical for the brotherhood Union is found in the 18th Chapter if Exodus and In Acts 7:38. They agreed.

The fourfold purpose of the brotherhood

(A) To deepen the spirituality of Men.
(B) To promote Religious Intelligence.
(C To cultivate Religious Fellowship.
(D) To win the loss to Christ.

He looked at them and they agreed. This was nothing new, they had heard all of this before. But this was the first time for many of them that they committed themselves to the purpose of what they stood for. He could tell by looking into the face of some of the members that they wondered why did the deacons have to commit to what the brotherhood stand for. He looked at them until it began to soak in. The deacons are a part of the church, they are not going anywhere, their families, their jobs are in this community. He wanted the membership to be proud and respect the deacons.

He wanted them to give praise of appreciating. He wanted the men to have respect for the membership, knowing that whatever comes up they can handle it.

A couple of the pastors were looking un-comfortable. There were something with the setup that they did not like. Then again it may have been moderator King, there were some who still did not like him and they could not hide it. There were some who did not care, their coming back were for the church, the church wanted fellowship with other churches. To believe that they were all on the same page, is a mistake. Rev. King said a silent prayer to his father. Smiled to himself, and spoke. "how many of you can tell me what the articles of Faith really is, and what are they about.? No one said a word. Finally one brother said, "It is the biblical guide line for us to live by." Another brother spoke up. "I don't know what each article means, but every leader, preacher and deacon should know what they mean, even if they don't remember each article."

Rev. King opened a book and began to read the articles to them. Then he stopped, "I want every member who becomes a member of one of the churches in our association to have three things: Baptist have historically used three official documents (A constitution,) (a covenant) and (articles of faith). The first provides for the orderly conduct of the church and its business. The second is a sacred agreement between the members of the church whereby they express their devotion to the Lord and to each other. The third sets forth clearly the doctrinal truth held by the members. He turned to the pastors, chairman of deacon board, listen to me carefully, make sure that every leader of your church, read and study all three of these before you come back to the convention in October. Nor only read them, but study them, you don't have to know them by heart, but know what they mean.

THE CHURCH CONSTITUTION.

The scriptures lay down broad principals concerning the church. It is clear that the officers are to be pastors and deacons with specific qualifications, and that they are chosen by the church. The method of their selection is left to the church, and need to be settled by each church to avoid confusion. The local church meets to transact its business, as illustrated in the disciplining of wayward members (Matt. 18:17; 1 Cor. 5.) The scriptures does not, however, give details as to how to determine who is qualified to vote in such a meeting. Clarity on this point is essential to internal harmony. What is the name of the church? How many deacons are to be elected? When is the annual meeting to be held? Who is qualified to serve as teachers?. These and many similar details are cot spelled out in the New Testament, but may be settled by consent of the members of a local church, in harmony with the principals of the Word of God. Such practical regulations are logically stated and preserved in an orderly manner in a constitution.

The Lord is a God of order, not of confusion, as evidenced in both creation and revelation. He has commanded us to do every decently and in order (1 Cor. 14:40.). A co situation, if drawn up wisely and prayerfully, is a major step toward order and decency in the conduct of a church. It should provide Biblical, ethical and orderly methods of business procedure. If these items are determined clearly in advance of the times when they may become problems, the solution can be calm and objective, and much friction and strife can be avoided.

Many churches have ignored their constitution through the years; thus no one knows where a copy can be found, or if one ever existed. Other churches have constitution that have not been revised in many decades and do not meet the problems current in our generation. Some church constitution were drawn up by leaders who do not hold baptistic, New Testament doctrine and practice.

Churches in any of the above situations will show real wisdom to appoint a committee to recommend any needed revisions, or to draw up a constitution if none is available.(The pastor should be a members of that committee.)

Such recommendations must be brought to the church for prayerful consideration and decision before they can be incorporated into the constitution for approval.

It will be wise for the committee to secure copies of constitutions from other sound Baptist Churches. Help may also be secured from the Department of Practical Theology in a sound Baptist college or seminary.

It may be well to consult a lawyer on some of the legal aspects to avoid serious future problems. For instance, In new york trustees in a Baptist church must number three, six, nine or twelve, and they must be elected in a corporate business meeting in which only members twenty-one years of age or older are allowed to vote. Furthermore, unless the church specifically provide that none can vote except active members of the church, the state law allows none members who attend or who support the church to vote in the corporate. Every constitution should protect the rights of the church members on this point. State laws vary, and each church is under obligation to conduct its business in a legal manner (Rom. 13)

The temptation is drawn up a new constitution or in revamping one is to consider the people involved rather than the Biblical principles. This is unsound and foolish. We must adhere to the word of God even if we offend people who are not subject to it. For Example, some churches have failed to require immersion for membership simply because one or more friends might not join the church because of this Biblical standard. Failure at this point allows the number of un-immersed members to multiply. Eventually there is a major division, and many members are lost. What is still more serious is that the church has compromised the truth, having feared the face of men more than the face of God.

Baptist are convinced that the word of God is the final authority in all matters of faith and conduct. This basic principal is not altered by the acceptance of a doctrinal statement and a constitution. These instruments are only the mutually agreed upon expression of the Biblical principals is a simple, condensed and accessible form.

We suggest the following constitution as a pattern to churches writing a constitution or remodeling an old one. Naturally, changes will need to be made to adapt to local situation. Some of these have been indicated by italics, such as the number of deacons, the size of the quorum, etc. These will vary with the size of the church, the convictions of the members and other factors.

Rev.\ King took a deep breath, looked out over the congregation, then he spoke, "We will not present the forms at this time.

But we will remember the words that we have spoken. we will remember then and follow them. I've noticed that we are getting short on time and we still have not covered the church Covenant. Pastors do not assign these three important principals to anyone except himself.

The article of faith with the scriptures where they are found, and a copy of the church covenant which they are bound by as a covenant between the member and the church, before God.

ARTICLES OF FAITH.

Each church need a clear statement of faith which sets forth great Biblical doctrines which it believes.

The article of Faith are not designed to be the foundation or the defense of our faith. They simply define and declares what we believe the word of God teaches on these vital doctrines.

The following is provided to assist churches which are preparing or revising their doctrinal statement.

The Scripture:

\1. We believe that the Holy Bible was written by men divinely inspired, and as a perfect treasure of heavenly instructions; that it had God for its author, salvation for its end, and truth without mixture of error for its matter, that it reveals the principals by which God will judge us, and there forth is, and shall remain to the end of the world, the true center of Christian Union, and the supreme standard by which all humans conduct, creeds and opinions shall be tried. (2 Tim. 3:16-17, 2 Peter 1:19-21)

II. The True God:

We believe the scriptures teach that there is one and only one, living and true God, an intelligent Spirit whose name is Jehovah, the maker and supreme ruled of heaven and earth; inexpressibly glorious in holiness, and worthy of all possible honor, confidence and love; that in the unity of the Godhead there are three persons, the father, the son, and the Holy Ghost; equal in every divine [perfection, and executing distinct but harmonious office in the great work of redemption. (Exod. 20:2-3; 1 Cor. 8:6, Rev. 4:11)

III The Fall of Man;

We believe the scriptures teach that men was created in holiness, under the law of his maker; but by voluntary transgression fell from that Holy and happy state; in consequence of which all mankind are now sinners, not by constraint but choice; being by nature utterly void of holiness required by the law of God, positively inclined to evil; and therefore under just condemnation to eternal ruin without defense or excuse. (Gen.3:1-6, Rom. 3:10-19, 5:12 and 19, 1:18-32

The Way of Salvation:

IV. \We believe that the scripture teach that the salvation of sinners is wholly of grace; through the mediatory offices of the son of God; who by the appointment of the father; freely took upon him our nature, yet without sin; honored the divine law by his personal obedience, and by his death made a full atonement for our sins, that have risen from the dead, he is now enthroned in heaven; and uniting in his wonderful person the tender sympathies with divine perfections, he is in every way qualified to be a suitable, a compassionate, and an all sufficient Savior.(Jonah:2:9, Eph, 2:8, Acts 15:11, Rom, 3:24-25, John 3:16 Matt. 18:11 Isa. 53:4-7, John 4:10, 1 Cor.15:3, Phil. 2:7-8.)

V. Justification.

We believe the scriptures teach that the great gospel blessings which Christ secures to such as believe in him is justification includes the pardon of sin; and the promise of eternal life on principals of righteousness; that is bestowed, not in consideration of any works of righteousness which we have done, but solely through faith in the redeemer's blood; by virtue of which faith is perfect righteousness is freely imputed to us of God; that it brings us into a state of most blessed peace and favor with God, and secures every other blessing needed for time and eternity. (Rom. 3:24, 4:5; 5:1, AND 9, Gal. 2:16 Phil 3:9.)

V1. Sanctification

We believe that Sanctification is the divine setting apart of the believer unto God, accomplished in a threefold manner, first, an eternal act of God, based upon redemption in Christ, establishing the believer in a position of holiness at the moment he trust the Savior; second, a continuing process in the saint as the Holy Spirit applies the word of God to the life; third, the final accomplishment of this process at the Lords return. (Heb. 10:10-14; 3:1; John 17:17; 2 Cor. 3:18; 1 Cor. 1:30; Eph. 5:25-27; 1 Thess.4:3-4; 5:23-24; 1 John 3:2; Jude 24, 25; Rev. 22:11)

V11. The Freeness of Salvation;

We believe the scriptures teach that the blessing of salvation are made free to all by the gospel; that it is the immediate duty of all to accept them by cordial, penitent and obedient faith; and that nothing prevents the salvation of the greatest sinner on earth, but his own determine depravity and voluntary rejection of the gospel, which rejection involves him in an Aggravated condemnation.

VII Regeneration;

We believe that the scriptures teach that in order to be saved, sinners must be regenerated, or born again; that regeneration consist of giving a Holy disposition to the mind; that it is affected in a manner above our comprehension by the power of the Holy Spirit, in connection with divine truth, so as to secure our voluntary obedience to the gospel; and that its proper evidence appears in the holy fruits of repentance and faith, and newness of faith.

VIII. Repentance and Faith;

We believe the scriptures teach that repentance and faith are sacred duties, and also inseparable graces, wrought in our souls by the regenerating Spirit of God; whereby being deeply convinced of our guilt, danger, and helplessness, and of the way of salvation, confession and supplication for mercy; at the same time heartily receiving the Lord Jesus Christ as our prophet savior, priest, and King, and relying on him alone as the only and all-sufficient Savior.

IX. God's Purpose of Grace;

We believe the scriptures teach that election is the eternal purpose of God, according to which he graciously regenerates, sanctifies and save sinners; that being perfectly consistent with the free agency of man, it comprehends all the means in connection of the end; that it is a glorious display of God's sovereign goodness, being infinitely free, wise, holy and unchangeable, that it utterly excludes boasting and promotes humility, love, prayer, praise, trust in God, and active imitation of his free mercy; that it encourages the use of means in the highest degree; that it may be ascertained by its efforts in all who truly believe the gospel; that it is the foundation of Christian assurance; and that to ascertain it with regard to ourselves demands and deserves the utmost diligence.

Resurrection and Priesthood of Christ

We believe in the bodily resurrection of Christ and in His

ascension into heaven, where He now sits at the right hand of the Father as our High Priest, interceding for us. (Matt. 28:6-7; Luke 24:39; John 20:27; 1 Cor. 15:4; Mark 16:6;Luke 24:2-6, 51; Acts 1:9-11; Rev. 3:21; Heb. 8:6; 12:2; 1 John 2:1; Heb 2:17; 5:10.)

The Devil, or Satan

We believe in the reality and personality of Satan, the Devil; and that he was created by God as an angel but through pride and rebellion became the enemy of his creator; that he became the unholy god of this age and the ruler of all the powers of darkness and is destine to the judgment of an eternal justice in the lake of fire. Matt. 4:1-11; 2 Cot. 4:4; Rev. 20:10)

X. Sanctification;

We believe the scriptures teach that sanctification is the process by which, according to the will of God, we are made partakers of his holiness; that it is a progressive work; that it is begun in regeneration; and that it is carried on in the heart of believers by the presence and power of the holy spirit, the sealer and comforter, in the continual use of the appointed, means especially the word of God, self-examination, self-denial, watchfulness, and prayer.

X1. Perseverance of Saints.

We believe the scriptures teach that such only are real believers as endure to the end; that their perseverance and attachment to Christ is the grand mark with distinguishes them from superficial professors that a special providence watches over their welfare ; and they are kept by the power of God, self-examination, self-denial, watchfulness, and prayer.

XII. The Law and Gospel;

We believe that the scriptures teach that the law of God is the eternal and unchangeable rule of his moral government; that it is holy, just, and good; and that the inability which the scriptures ascribe to fallen men to fulfill its precepts, arise entirely from their love of sin; to deliver them from which, and to restore them through a mediator to unfeigned obedience to the holy law, is one great end of the gospel, and of the means of grace connected with the establishment of the visible church.

XIII. A Gospel Church;

We believe the scriptures teach that a visible church of Christ is a congregation of baptized believers, associated by covenant in the faith and fellowship of the Gospel, observing the ordinances of Christ; govern by his laws; and exercising the gifts, rights, and privileges invested in them by His Word, that its only scriptural officers are bishop or pastors, and deacons whose qualification, claims and duties are defined in the Epistles to Timothy and Titus.

We believe the true mission of the church is the faithful witness of Christ to all men as we have opportunity. We hold that the local church has been absolute right of self-government, free from the interference of any hierarchy of individuals or organizations; and that the one and only Superintendent is Christ through the Holy Spirit; that it is scriptural for true churches to cooperate with each other in contending for the faith and for the furtherance of the gospel; that each local church is the sole judge of the measure and method of its cooperation; that on all matters of membership, or polity, of government, of discipline, of benevolence, the will of the local church is final. (1 Cor. 11:2, ACTS 20:17028, 1 Tim. 3:1-13 Acts 2:41-41)

We believe in the unity of all New Testament believers in the Church which is the body of Christ. 1 Cor. 12:12-13, Eph. 1:22-23, 3:1-6,4:11, 5:23; Col.1:18 Acts 15:13-18

XIV. Baptism and The Lord Supper;

We believe that Christian baptism is the single immersion of a believer in water to show forth in a solemn and beautiful emblem our identification with the crucified, buried and risen Savior, through whom we died to sin and rose to a new life; that baptism is to be performed under the authority of the local church; and that it is prerequisite to the privilege of church members.

We believe that the Lord's supper is the commemoration of Hid death until He come, and should be preceded always by solemn self-examination.

We believe that the Biblical order of the ordinances is baptism first and then the Lord Supper, and that participants in the Lord's Supper should be immersed believers. (Acts 8:36, 38, 39; John 3:33; Roman 6:3-5; Matt.3:16; Co. 2:12; 1 Cor. 11:23-28; Matt. 28:19-20.

Separation

We believe in obedience to the Biblical commands to separate ourselves unto God from worldliness and ecclesiastical apostasy. (2 Cor. 6:14-7:1; 1 Thess. 1:9, 10; 1 Tim.6:3-5; Rom. 16:17 2 John 1:9-11.)

XV. THE Christian Sabbath;

We believe the scriptures teach that the first day of the week is the Lords Day, or the Christian Sabbath and is to be kept sacred to religious purposes, by abstaining from all secular labor, both private and public, and by preparation for the rest that remained for the people of God.

XVI Civil Government;

We believe that the scriptures teach the civil government, for the interest and good order of human society; and that magistrates are to be prayed for, conscientiously honored and obeyed, except only in things opposed to the will of our Lord Jesus Christ, who is the only Lord of the conscience, and the coming King of Kings. (Rom. 13:1-7; 2 Sam.23:3; exod.18:21, 22; Acts 23:5; Matt.22:21; Acts 5:2: 4:19, 20; Dan. 3:17-18.)

The Virgin Birth

We believe that Jesus was begotten of the Holy Spirit in a miraculous manner, born of Mary, a virgin, as no other man was ever born or can be born of woman, and that He is both the Son of God and God the Son. (Gen. 3:15; Isa. 7:14; Matt. 1:18-26; Luke 1:35; John 1:14.)

XVII. Righteous and Wicked;

We believe that the scriptures teach that there is a radical and essential difference between the righteous and the wicked; that such only as through faith are justified in the name of the Lord Jesus, and sanctified by the spirit of our God, are truly righteous in his esteem; while all such as continue in impenitence and unbelief are in his sight wicked, and under the curse; and his distinction holds among men both in and after death, (128) in the everlasting felicity of the saved and the everlasting conscious suffering of the lost in the lake of fire.(Mal.3:18;; Gen. 18:23; Rom. 6:17, 18; 1 John 5:19; Rom. 7:6; 6:23; Prov. 14:32; Luke 16:25;Matt. 25:34-41; John 8:21; Rev.20:14-15)

XVIII. The World To Come;

We believe that the scriptures teach that the end of the world is approaching; that at the last day, Christ will descend from heaven, and raise the dead from the grave, and for final retribution; that a solemn separation will take place; that the wicked will be judged to endless punishment, and the righteous to endless joy; and that this judgment will fix forever the final state of men in heaven or hell, on principals of righteousness.

The other instrument is the church covenant.

Rapture and Subsequent Events.

We believe that Christ will return for the church in the middle of the tribulation period. This event could occur at any moment, and that at that moment the dead in Christ shall be given glorified bodies without tasting death, and all should be caught up to meet the Lord in the air before the seven years of Tribulation (1Thess. 4:13-18; 1 Cor. 15:42-44, 51-54; Phil. 3:20-21; Rev. 3:10)

We believe that the Tribulation, which follows the Rapture of the church, will be culminated by the revelation of Christ in in power and great glory to set upon the throne of David and to establish the millennial kingdom (Dan. 9:25-27; Matt.24;29-31; Luke 1:30-33; Isa. 9:6-7; 11:1-9; Acts 29:29, 30; Rev.20:1-4, 6)\

Israel

We believe in the sovereign selection of Israel as God's eternal covenant people, that she is now dispersed because of her disobedience and rejection of Christ, ant she will be re-gathered in the Holy Lands and, after the completion of the Church, will be saved as a nation at the second advent of Christ (Gen. 13:14-17; Rom. 11:1032; Ezek. 37.)

There will be some strange looks on faces in the crowd, some will be almost lost in not knowing what is being said. The churches have not done a good job of teaching their members what they are to believe. Rev. King was feeling his way around the subject matter.

He did not want any infighting, no setting up some members against the others, he wanted this union to flow together. The work that lie ahead were too important to be snagged on a rock of misunderstanding. Some of these articles, some of you have studied, others, you have not. Some of these are not your conviction, but they are what we believe as a association. It will help keep us together, traveling down the same road in Godly love. Let me give you an example; Some believe that Christ will return at the beginning of the Tribulation. There are others who believe that he will take the church at the middle of the Tribulation, giving the church a last time to become obedient; to repent of their sins. And still there are others who believe that he will come after the church at the end of the Seven Year Tribulation period. Your salvation will not be weighed upon either of these. The warning is clear, be ready, we don't know when he is coming, but we know that he is coming.

He kind of raised his head with a small smile on his face. He was thankful to God for getting him out of this situation. Now he had to turn to another simple, but problem area. Is the not keeping the covenant a sin? Then he turned and asked it another way; Is it a sin to disobey the church covenant? He saw from his position the bowing and the shaking of the head through out the audience. There were a little verbal disagreement in one to two spots in the sanctuary. At one time it had gotten kind of noisy, and tempers were rising. This in part was what he wanted and needed. Now he could take his time and share with them what the association was teaching the churches. We are not trying to change what you believe, neither are we trying to cause you to think in a different way. But check the scriptures for your final answer. But as far as the Association is concern we will keep these three documents, and they will help to keep us together. He knew that when they walked our of the building, there were some who was not going to believe; but he anted them to work together in love.

He offered a ten minute break than they were coming back together to finish the studies on this information. When they had returned, they began on the Church Covenant.

Church Covenant

Having been led by the Holy Spirit to receive the Lord Jesus Christ as our savior, and on the public confession of our faith, (130) having been immersed in the name of the Father, and of the Son, and of the Holy Ghost, we do now, in the presence of God and this assembly solemnly and joyfully enter into covenant with one another, as one body in Christ.

We purpose, therefore, by the aid of the Holy Spirit, to walk together in Christian love; to strive for the advancement of this church in knowledge, holiness and comfort; to promote its prosperity and spirituality ; to attend its services regularly; to sustain its worship, ordinances, discipline and doctrine; to give it a sacred preeminence over all institutions of human origin; to give faithfully of time and talent in its activities; to contribute cheerfully and regularly, as

God has prospered us, to the support of the ministry, the expenses of the church, the relief of the poor, and the spread of the gospel throughout all nations.

We also purpose to maintain family and private devotion; to train our children according to the word of God; to seek the salvation of our kindred and acquaintances; to walk circumspectly in the world; to be just in our dealings, faithful in our engagements, an exemplary in our conduct; to avoid all gossip, backbiting, and unrighteous; to abstain all forms of activity--including the sale and use of intoxicating beverage -which dishonor out Lord Jesus Christ, cause stumbling to a fellow believer or hinder the winning of souls to Christ; to be zealous in our efforts to advance the cause of Christ, our savior and to give him preeminence in all things.

We further purpose to encourage one another in the blessed hope of our Lord's return; to watch over one another in brotherly love; to remember each other in prayer; to aid each other in sickness and distress ; to cultivate Christian sympathy in feeling and courtesy in speech; to be slow to take offense, but always ready for reconciliation, and, mindful of the rules of our savior, to seek it without delay.

We moreover purpose that when we remove from this place we will soon as possible unite with some other church of like faith and order where we can carry out the spirit of this covenant and the principles of God's word. If there is no such church, we shall seek, with the Lord's help, to establish one.

The moderator stood there for a while, thinking about all that had been said here tonight. Hoping that no one would get a misunderstanding. Hoping that all the churches represented in this group of those who are graduating into the Cap/Rock District Association, will feel a pride in their moderator and the association.

He looked at his watch and then moved on. Each of you will be given a policy card, that you should carry with you where ever you go. I am going to read the policy, if you do not agree, at the end say so.

Regard for leadership

Undergirding the whole program of the church.

The respect of the rights of others.

The absolute duty of each brother to Live a Christian life.

The necessity of temperance.

The obligation of every brother to us his talents and The opportunity to develop his faculties.

To deepen Spirituality.

To promote religious intelligence and to lead the lost to Christ.

There came another hesitation, this time with a frown on his face. His mind was back at the graduation, it was hard for him to turn it loose. He took his pad, turned it over, and pushed it away from him. Everyone was watching him carefully. Surely there were nothing else to discuss with the graduation, they were about tired of hearing him talk. He had not lost them, they had grown tired of so much that had fallen upon them so quickly. He looked at the pad laying on the corner of the rostrum, then he walked away three or four feet, then turned and faced them.

"It seem to me that this group of people are committed to the will of God. Each brother will now take turns and share with the church that you will lead, how you know that you have been born again. Give us a definition on what true repentance mean. How do you know that you have the love of God within you. And what communication have you had with God to make you know that your calling is into leadership. One out of every five brothers will speak for five minutes, and in that five minutes make a strong point, to show that you know who God is in your life.

This caught the brothers by surprise and one brother, who most church members looked at as being kind of "dumb" stepped forward.

"In the book of Luke the fifty chapter, it states that Jesus was sharing early one morning, and when people came upon him to the point that he could go no further backward, he looked over and saw men washing their nets. He asked one Simon Peter if he could use his boat to finish sharing the gospel. When he was through, he told them to cast their nets into the deep and they could catch much fish.

One Simon said to him, "We have fished here all night and have not caught a thing, but nevertheless by you word we will obey.

When they had dropped their nets into the deep they caught more fish than they could pull to shore by themselves. They called for some help from the banks, they had caught so much fist. When the fish had been brought to shore, they forsook all and followed Jesus". Then he thanked them and sat down. There were three in all that spoke and the rest of them told how they knew that they had been born again. Some talked about true repentance, others how they knew that the love of God resides in their heart.

An older brother who walked on two canes, a very dark old brother, who had forgotten what teeth had been used for. He was bent, and seem to be in some pain. But with pride he set his face toward Jesus Christ and spoke; "For I received of the Lord that which I also handed on to you, that the Lord Jesus, on the night of which he was being delivered up, took bread, and, after he had given thanks, broke it and said, 'This is my body which is for you; this do that you may remember me'.

In that same hour, after the meal, he took the cup and said 'THIS CUP IS THE NEW COVENANT AND IT COST MY BLOOD. Do this, as often as you drink it, so that you will remember me' for as often as you eat this bread and drink this cup you do proclaim the d death of the Lord until he will come. Therefore whoever eats this bread and drink this cup of the Lord in an unfitting way is guilty of a sin against the body and blood of the Lord. But let a man examine himself, and so let him eat of that bread and drink of that cup. For he who eats and drinks as some of you do, eats and drinks judgment to himself, because he does not discern what the body mean. It is because of this that many among you are ill and weak and some have died. But if we truly discerned what we are like we would not be liable to judgment. But in this very judgment of the Lord we are being disciplined that we may not be finally condemned alone with the world." (I Cor. 11:23-32)

He folded his bible of which he did not have. Put the imaginary bible under his arm, then he smiled and looked up toward the people in the audience. "No passage in the whole new testament is of greater interest than this.

For one thing, it gives us our warrant for the most sacred act of worship in the Church. The Sacrament of the Lords Supper; and, for another since the letter to the Corinthians is earlier than the earliest of the gospels, this is actually the first recorded account we possess of any word of Jesus." He studied himself onto his cane and hobbled back to his seat. That proud look was still on his face, even though he was hurting, shaking and crippled. One could tell that the old man really loved the lord with all his heart, mind and soul.

One of the pastors came forward to explain Luke 9:21-22, 22-24. Jer. 9:23-24. Eph. 3:20. Joshua 1:7-9 and Heb. 6:4. The moderator again came forward and asked if there were any questions. When there were no questions, the moderator stood with his head down. Then he raised his head and asked a question. "Is it a sin to disobey the church covenant. Can we disregard the church covenant and read it like any other piece of literature. Will God hold us responsible for not teaching our people the meaning of the covenant that we have agreed to uphold. Let us just look at a verse or two.

Having been led by the Holy Spirit to receive the Lord Jesus Christ as our savior, and on the public confession of our faith, having been immersed in the name of the Father, and of the Son, and of the Holy Ghost, we do now, in the presence of God and this assembly, solemnly and joyfully enter into this covenant with one another as one body in Christ.

\We purpose, therefore, by the aid of the Hoy Spirit, to walk together in Christian love; to strive for the advancement of this church in knowledge, holiness and comfort; to promote its prosperity and spirituality; to attend its service regularity; to sustain its worship. When the last question was asked and answered; they put their bibles and notebooks down Rev. King observed the crowd, there were some serious concerns, but now was not the time to discuss them. Now is the time to close out, Have a late night knack, read their bibles and pray, yes pray and listen for God's response. They put their books aside and stood up, The youngest deacon in the group stood and gave the closing prayer. Each pastor, preacher, deacon was given three books, which is the foundation of this district association. The Holy Bible

the King James version and a copy of the living bible to assist in their study. The Brother Up Next-Braxton King.

The administration and Doctrine of the

Church-Paul R. Jackson. There are other books you may purchase for your study, but we want to make sure that you have these books, they will be used to help build a strong D.A. and bring pride to this area. Then they walked out on the same song that they marched in on. Each pastor and deacons will lead their congregation from the sanctuary to the parking lot.

END OF RE-VERSE MARRIAGE.

OK.

King sat there, in another man's house with a feeling of accomplishment. In one week he had touched four people who was dedicated to the cause. Within two weeks the other three people were identified. All three of these people were communicators, teachers and net working specialist. The concept of the D.A. was taught to the seven people thatRev. King was sure that God had shown him. The other five persons came aboard when they heard about a change in the D.A., they were not sure who was leading the ship, but they wanted to be on board. Of the five, three had been spoken to by the heavenly father and when they talked to Rev. King, he was sure that they were the people God wanted for this purpose. The last two he did not feel so comfortable with. They had the resources and time to travel without going into the budget. He quickly found out that they were getting information from the state who appointed Rev. King for this task. This was not a conflict, but he knew that what was being said went back to the state.

Rev. King had a brain storm two weeks later and called the seven together for a meeting. The meeting was held in a small town (East of San Antonio, called Seguin.) It was to be a three day meeting and every person had an assignment to be ready at the meeting. From this meeting they were to meet with the state, to make sure that they were in the same ball park. When they left the presence meeting, Rev. King was sure that this is what he was going forward with. He knew that some of the things that was discussed would not be taken to the meeting with the state. But would be a part of his plan for the D.A. He was aware that some people from the state only wanted him to lay a foundation, then they were going to remove him and put their people into leadership positions. He had gotten the word that they was going to disbar him from the District association and the state convention all together.

It was then that he decided to go all the way with his program, regardless what the state wanted. If he could move fast enough with churches that was hurt, The one's that have no ties with the state, his success with these churches could seal his position with the D.A. He knew that they had to move fast, the word was getting around that he had something up his sleeve.

The following month was jammed with teaching and discussing the principals of the new D.A. Since they had already decided on the material, and it was printed in the three books spoken of above, that made it easier to discuss. The plan was that the first three churches that was to return, would go through the marriage of believers. If that worked out to be successful, he was on his way. At the meeting at Seguin five churches would be the first to meet with the new D.A. There would be at least one or the original seven in the group to sit down and discuss the possibility of them coming back to the D.A. When they got to the meeting, their contact was so good that the report was, all five churches would come back into the fold. What impressed the churches most, was that the D.A. offered to train the churches in their home town and home church. They were to learn how to share the gospel with the loss. They were taught to know what it was that God wanted them to do. They learned about the finance of the church and how they were expected to gain financial independence for their obedience to God's word--Stewardship was taught with group of learners.

The catch that caught most churches was a phase that many churches had over looked. Until now conflict resolution was something that they read over without trying to understand its contents. The brother who has labored to prepare himself for the responsibility of becoming a deacon must understand the harsh misunderstanding of conflict resolution. This brother must understand that some conflicts are simple minor nuisances that we accept as natural components of existence. Others keep our relationship from realizing their full potential, and some become so severe that they do irreparable damage to individuals, families, workplaces, and entire communities. Learning how to deal with conflict effectively is increasingly an essential life skill needed by every person, leader and every group regardless of one's age, social role, profession, culture background, or belief.

These churches found out that the D.A. cared about them and they had a voice in the association. They learned about the books that the association was teaching,

The administration and Doctrine of the church by Paul. R. Jackson/The Brother up Next by Braxton King And of course the Holy Bible. It was made clear that faith in Jesus Christ, and obedience to the word of God was what was required for success on earth and a place in heaven for one's soul.

One of the assignment that was to brought to the meeting was a list of all the churches, those that has been and is presently a part of the association. Liz knew so many of the women throughout the state, the one's that she did not know sis. Hinton knew from way-back. She spent night and day on the phone calling the churches that she had on her list. She was asking them if they would be interesting in listening to the new program from the leadership of Rev. King. who most of the people respected. Rev. King had made some changes and the rest of the group had agreed with him. Instead of three or four things that is to be presented, put together a solid program idea that would strengthen the church and the association. Rev. King had remembered a program that he had witnessed a few months ago. A local church was having their 15th year church anniversary. The title: "Committed To Becoming A Great Church." He decided to use this same concept to organize his plan around.

He was to visit these five churches before the meeting in Seguin, Texas. He took with him Bro. Holmes, Sis Liz, Bro walker and Rev. Hinton. At each church they talked with the pastor and the deacon board, they found out that most of the deacons knew little about the association. Most of them really did not care. For to them it was a preacher's thing, a money thing and a power thing, and they did not want to be considered for this relationship. All five of the pastors were interesting in becoming a part of a spiritual group that could help their church.

That could excite their people and put them in the word of God for meaning.

The pastor of the church visited let his deacons know that he thought that the association was good for the church. But he made sure that they knew that the power of the church is in the membership. He asked them if they would listen to the association with an open mind. They agreed that something had to happen, because the churches were in demise, and people were walking away. Many said that they would never come back again. Some men divorced their wives because she remained with the church.

Rev. King had listen at all of the churches as the pastor had put a favorable role on their return to the association. If the truth was known, Rev. King had talked with the pastors before this meeting.

If he had not gotten a favorable reaction from the pastor, he would have moved on. There were only five deacons to this church and they had their suit and tie on. They looked like deacons, they acted like deacons, they would hold a deacon man conversation. They were proud to be deacons and knew what their qualifications were. There were no laughing and kidding around, this meeting was strictly business. There wives were there. but they were in another room. The women did not have anything to say at this time. There would be a time when they would be asked to share their opinions.

Rev. King was sitting to where he was facing the pastor and deacons of one of the churches. He shared with them, the first thing that we did and is doing is create an organizational chart. This chart is designed to tell all members of the church or organization where we are going for the next twenty five years. We know the talent, ability, and spiritual gifts that is needed for growth. We know what ministries we can handle at this time, and the one's we need to build toward. All members can look at the chart, and know where they belong. They know what ministries are available to practice and become a part of for the future. They know the head of each department and how to contact them. People will give more generously when they know where they are going. They will make more sacrifices to help the church and themselves. This chart will help the membership get an idea of what God is requiring at this church.

The organizational chart is the first instrument that the association will require. Many churches are not familiar with this chart, but we will train every church that desires to learn. This instruments carry the most wait, because it gives the membership clear direction. Of the path that we will be following. The next, God given instrument of direction is the purpose of the association. The purpose is to help men and women, and leaders how to practice their maturity to convince the membership that talk alone will not help us grow. What we need is practicing the word of God that we have learned and understood. Pleasing God make it clear that we may not get to heaven any other way.

CHAPTER # 10

Purpose of the association

He might be a vessel unto honor, sanctified, meet
for the master's use. (11Tim. 2:21)

We want every brother to know what the purpose of any organization,
that he is involved with.

After the chart has been prepared and the operational blocks
have been filled. Knowing the purpose of the association is a must.

We will not be able to move forward unless we know what the
purpose of this great task is all about. Pastor, when it comes to this
organization and its success, you can call me at any hour and ask me
any question concerning this great responsibility.

With these two pieces put together, our knowledge of what
we are doing has settled in our mind, we must then take on the
third responsibility, that is counting the cost. We sometime miss
directions from God because, because we do not yield to his word.
Let us look at Luke 14:26-30 NIV. "If anyone come to me and does
not hate his father and mother, his wife and children, his brother and
sisters,-yes, even his own life--he cannot be my disciple. Any anyone
who does not carry his cross and follow me cannot be my disciples.
Suppose one of you want to build a tower. Will he not first sit down
and estimate the cost to see if he has enough money to complete it,
for if he lays the foundation and is not able to finish it, everyone one

who sees it will ridicule him, saying this fellow began to build and was not able to finish."

Many leaders in today's church's have failed their congregation, because when a plan is presented, it is looked at as either good or bad. Few pastors will set down with his people and count the cost. They must know what the condition is for success. They must discuss what It will cost them if they go through with this plan. With a church involved, they must know the consequence of failure.. Because failure in one thing can doom the whole church if the plan is not thought out. It can cause members to lose confidence in the leadership. Failure of a large program, such as building fund, can shake the believability of a community in that church. When that happens, many people from that community do not want anything to do with that church.

Moderator, the three things that we have discussed; Organizational chart, purpose of the program and the cost of failure or success. We want all of our churches to be tied into what we are doing. We want them to enjoy the benefits of being obedient to God. Before we go on, there is a small box on the chart I want your opinion. I am thinking about a small box to the side of the chart, where that committee will report directly to me. I know that this is a dangerous step, but it is a need that should be covered.

In almost every church there is a family member who attend church and one who do not. I am talking primary about wives who attend and husbands who do not. I know, I know, I know this is a touchy situation and there are dangerous every where in this road. But I think that a ministry geared toward the unsaved person in the house is worth the risk. They will get extensive training, from professional who have had experience in this field. We will take the committee And let them help us to train others. This will be done before we go out into the community teaching other churches.

The pastor's wife knocked on the door. She asked if they wanted some coffee. Every body in the room was ready for some hot coffee. There were smiles all over the room./ It may not have been apparent before, but it certainly was now, that a break was needed. The pastor seem to be a little uncertain about something that Rev. King had said. "Something troubling you pastor," As he sipped his coffee. He got up and went to the window, but he was not looking out the window, he was looking into his own soul. A soul that sometime lay bare with only enough substance to keep it functional. Somewhere in the back of his mind, lingering at the top of his

soul, his conscious cried out for companionship, of a soul that knew God personally. He stood there trying to find our if the Lord was saying something to him. This new association was different from anything that he knew about. Some of what was said he had not heard, and he did not know what to think of it. At times he understood counting the cost, and at other times he did not. One thing was for sure, he did not know how to install it in his church. Just to know that someone will be available to assist him, made him feel good.

Rev. King thanked his host for the coffee, and they all sat down to continue the conversation. King looked at Liz and nodded his head. Liz began by saying that the association could help build the church through three principals. The pastor knew her better than the others that sat in on the conversation. He smiled at her, "You know me and my church better than anyone in the room. Apparently you know this concept better than most of the people in the room. I don't believe that you would be here if you didn't

think this program would help us." Pastor you are absolutely right, if I did not think that this plan can and will help our people I would not be here. There are a couple of parts left.

Liz began to talk about the three principals. The first one is: The great confession--Matthew 16:15-16.kjv. "He said unto them, But whom say ye that I am? And Simon Peter answered and said, thou art the Christ, the son of the living God." "When man want to know concerning his spiritual lied, even his salvation, the best place to go is our heavenly father. Flesh and blood does not supply, man and books does not supply the answer. Jesus says that my father who is in heaven, is able to supply our spiritual needs.

The next is the Great Commandment--Matthew 22:37-40.kjv "Jesus said unto him, thou shalt love the lord thy God with all thy heard, and with all thy soul, and with all thy mind. This is the first and great commandment. And the second is like unto it, they shall love thy neighbor as thyself. On these two commandments hang all the law and the prophets." She said, "There is a principal in progress that we want to attach to this truth. When a person rededicate their lives, or come back to the church, some time from backsliding and others from just being away. Two strong, mature Christians brothers or sisters should take them to a room provided for this purpose. If they have backsliding, bring them back to their faith in Christ Jesus. See if the Love of God has found enough faithfulness for Christ to rule and abide. Talk to them before they are allowed to leave the building.

The third principal is, The Great Commission--Matthew 28:19-20. "Go ye therefore, and teach all nations, baptizing them in the name of the father, and of the Son, and of the Holy Ghost: Teaching them to observe all things whatsoever I have commanded you: and, lo, I am with you always, even unto the end of the world. Amen." Then she said, "Pastor the teaching that the association will be doing is a little foreign to me. With all honesty, I have not grasped the heart and soul of its concept. I have to admit that some of it is hard to swallow, and to accept it at face value, is a little frightening. Pastor King has said that God gave it to him, but, maybe he is still working on me."

Rev. King said, "Let all of us get into this discussion. Let each of us be truthful with what he believes. Now is the time to speak out, let us try to cover every area that we can think about." He went on to say that before Jesus left to go back to his father he left us a command. Just one, that's Matthew 28:19-20, The scripture that Sis Liz were talking about a moment ago.

But there is another scripture that has been in the bible since the cover was installed. It says the same thing in another way. Look closely at the words that Mark speak, it more like instructions than a command. It makes some things clear, but it also make some Christians uneasy. This scripture challenges their faith in action and works.

Look at Mark 16:15-18 (NIV). He said to them, "Go into all the world, and preach the good news to all creation. Whoever believes and is baptized will be saved, but whoever does not believe will be condemned. And these signs will accomplish those who believe.: In my name they shall drive out demons; they will speak in new tongues: They will pick up snakes with their hands; And when they drink deadly poison, it will not hurt them at all; they will place their hands on the sick, and they will get well." This is the great commission. But it breaks some practical things down, so that we can practice them. Both of these scriptures are the same. They say the same thing to all believers. But they give believers a total point of view that causes some people to hide in fear. And it causes some travelers to take a different road, that leads to fear and doubt. But whatever we think, it does not change God's word. God expects obedient to his word, no excuses, no reason for failure, except disobedience.

Rev. King had been standing at the window for a long time, he did not seem to be looking for anything specific Finally in front of him on the window seal was a pencil sharpen on both ends, and then twice in the middle. Outside the window, on the ground, a raven and a dove stood looking up at him. For the first time he could see their eyes./; Their eyes was brown, and it seem as if they were trying to smile. Quickly the Eagle came in a dive, he hesitated in mid-air for a small second, then he went up, straight up until he was out of sight. When Rev. King looked back to the ground, his little friends were gone.. It was then that he noticed that the pencil had disappeared and he felt all alone, It frighten him at first, then his friends in the room was back where they were before. Sis. Hinton, was troubled by the expression on his face. Then she said, "Do you want us to pray?" Without turning around he said, " every thing is going to be all right. I have received the promise from above. All is well."

Rev. King raised his head and caught the pastor by the hand. He shared with him the love of the Lord that had brought them together. How they must stay together, worshiping God in the middle of their understanding of the word of God. He went back and quoted Matthew 28:19-20. Pastor here is what we will teach and believe. Because we believe it to be true and what God wants us to share with those who have fallen away. But you know, it is true, and because it is true, it may be hard to understand and believe, but either way it is true.

He went on to say that when Jesus was getting ready to leave, he left one commandment, that is the Great Commission. We don't always need to know why of everything, it is our responsibility to obey. You remember when Jesus chose the twelve? He realized that he was the only one who had the true message. He chose twelve and taught them the message, while they were with him here on earth. If he had not, who was going to deliver a message they did not believe. He taught them all that his father had given him. And now after he had carried out the plan that the father had given him, he left them a command, go yea therefore.

"Pastor, it seem to be clear to me, and I want to see what you think about this revelation. A command from Jesus is instructions from Jesus that he wants his family to obey. If they refuse to obey after they had read and understood his desire toward them, then it is a sin when they disobey. The great commission when believed, become a un-repented sin in the life of the believer. This un-repented sin is only forgiver able when the person that has disobeyed in the face of God; will confess his sin of disobedience, by naming the sin and promising God that he will not be disobedient to God in this matter. This un-repented sin must be confessed and turned away from. Then it will not be a sin to that believer, The believer will leave his knees being obedient to God and his word.

If the believer disagrees that disobeying the Great Commission is a sin, the sin of disobeying God will never leave him until he repent. Then the sin of disobedience will be upon him, un-repented. This sin does not go away because we ask God to forgive us all of our sins. It will only Go away when we repent of the sin. Many people walk around every day believing that God has forgiven them, when in fact he has not. Un-repented sin of disobeying the Great Commission may linger with us, and keep us defeated as a Christian for a long time. Many Christian people live a defeated life, unknown to them that they are being defeated. In this defeat stage of their lives, they welcome Satan into their life to live with them.

He will live there until you become aware of God's command, and say Yes Lord, to the command's direction to share the gospel. You must be aware that there is no other way to share the gospel except through other believers. If you are not a believer, you cannot share the gospel of Jesus Christ. You can tell the story, but you can't share the word.

"Pastor you are aware that in these last days, the church has wondered away from God. It has moved away slowly, bringing more of the world into it, then it is convincing the world to come into the church. At a time when the church should be saturating the world with its witnesses; sharing the gospel of Jesus Christ. It is lingering alone cripple with worldly music, praising those who raise the roof with their emotional out burst. We get emotional, shout, hollering and speaking in tongues or a dialect that is not words, but something to fool the people. We have become a show, with no substances or true direction for the people who has come to worship. We must go back to our basis. We must find roots that have a solid foundation that can hold us in a time of difficulty. We are in a time that the church must be obedient to God's word. And God said go ye, and share the gospel. but we feel as if we can get into heaven as we are. We think that because God is a loving God, merciful God, a patient God, a God who forgives that we can run over Him, but not so.

The church has fallen away from the old school of Christian living. The concept of witnessing, or sharing to convince the lost to accept Jesus or reject him is now old foggy. Why? The church has forgotten who Jesus Christ is. Oh, they read about him in books even the Bible, but they don't know him. They know the story, but they don't know him, they believe some of the things that is said in the Bible is true. But they don't believe all of it, they just can't believe that all of it is the word of God. They say, how can one be all three, and all three is one, to them it does not make sense. But to those who have sold out to the cross, it is clear and wonderful news. I think that the concept that once saved is always saved, helps Satan more than anything else. Without an explanation we will live in an a backsliding state without any desire to repent. Our thought is that the life we are living is good enough to get us into heaven. Yes, Yes Our main problem is we have forgotten who God is. We have forgotten who Jesus Christ is and what he has done for us. Let us look for a brief moment and see if we can remember who our savior really is.

Some time ago Jesus was walking with the twelve down around the coast Caesarea of Philippi. He noticed that the men he had taught personally, had some doubt, and maybe a little fear. There were things that they did not understand. They did not understand how he was going to die, stay in the grave three days, then rise up and return to the father alive. So he asked them, "Who do men say that I the son of man is." They responded, some say you are Jeremiah, some John the Baptist, and others say one of the prophets. Simon Peter spoke out, "Thy art the Christ the son of the living God." Jesus said to him. "Simon, flesh and blood did not reveal that to you, but my father in heaven" If we want to know spiritual things ask the father. He will never fail us or forsake us. He is always available to assist us in all things that a Christian is in need of.

Let us look back at what peter said, "Thy art the Christ the son of the living God." look what Jesus said, "Flesh and blood did not reveal this to you, but my father who is in heaven.". Let us look at two scriptures which shed some light on what Jesus was saying. In the book of Mark 4:12 NIV. "They may be ever seeing but never perceiving, and even hearing but never understanding, otherwise they might turn and be forgiven" Let us look at another scripture that you will need to hear from heaven. Mark 10:12-14. " The next day as they were leaving Bethany, Jesus was hungry. Seeing in the distant a fig tree in leaf, he went to find out if it had any fruit. When he reached it, he found nothing be leaves, because it was not the season for figs. Then he said to the tree, 'May no one ever eat fruit from you again.' and his disciples heard him say it." These two scriptures are not easy to understand. The best advice we can give come from the mouth of Jesus. Ask the father. There isn't anything that the believing brother can ask the father in the spirit that he will not share the truth.

Still traveling toward Jerusalem, teaching the twelve that he had chosen, preparing them to be ready when the time come for him to go back to be with his father. He stopped over at the Mount of Olives to pray. When he was in town, he always stopped over here to pray. He took his disciples to a certain place and told them to pray while he was gone. A little further, he told Peter, James and John to stay there and pray. He then went about a stone throw away and he kneeled down to pray. His prayed to the father to take this bitter cup from him, but not my will, he said, but your will be done. He prayed this prayer over and over again, making sure that God's will had to be done. The father already believed that his son had to go through this time of disappointment in his young life. He came back to his disciples and found them asleep, and asked them if they could not have stayed awake for one hour, then he told them to sleep on. He went back to his praying place and began to pray again. He prayed with such intensity until sweat like big drops of blood fell upon the ground. Heaven dispatched and angel to assist him; and then he prayed more earnestly-father if it is your will take this bitter cup from me, but not my will but your will be done. All of this he done for us, even his suffering.

Later on, on his journey to Calvary, he entered the city. There is where he was betrayed, but soon after this ordeal, they were trying to make up their mind what to do with him. His people carried him to a small dim room at night, and when they came out, they wanted him crucified. For they said that, he said that he was the son of God. On his way to the cross many people saw him for who he was. They may not have understood all things, but they believed in him.

They nailed him to the cross, it was an old rugged cross that they drove the large nails through his hands, and he never said a mumbling word.

They raised him from the ground and stood him between heaven and earth. Earth did not want him, for they said crucify him; heaven could not receive him for he had finished what he had come for. Hanging there on the cross, innocent of no sin or crime, he pained from his mothers side, unbearable pain. But then at twelve o'clock, it became dark. There were no light no where in the world. The moon refused to shine, the stars did not twinkle and the sun hid itself and refused to shine.

The darkness, was so dark that one could reach out and catch it between their fingers. There were no room to move about, for the darkness covered the whole earth. Their fingers when they reached them out could feel a heavy nothingness that was the darkness all around them. No light in the created world anywhere. They tell me that at this time Jesus became sin for mankind. He did not sin, he was never disobedient, he done no wrong. He obeyed his father unto and after death. He became sin for us-he did not sin, but he became sin for us. He then cried out FATHER WHY HAST THY FORSAKEN ME. Then he dropped his head in the lock of his shoulders and said that it was finished. Into thy hands I command my spirit, He gave up the (fight)and went to the grave, for a three day stay. He got up, saw many before he went back to be with the father. Before he went back to his father he left us a command, and that was to go tell the world the good news. That through him, every person has a chance to eternal life.

Look at us now, we have forgotten who he is. Pastor, Rev. King said, "We are looking for three persons to fill out the seven that we need at the heart of this movement. You have never been liked by leadership. They have talked about you, criticize you for almost every thing that you do. What you believe, you stood by what the word of God said. Your daughter is cut from the same cloth, what she believe she stands by it. I remember when she graduated from college, her minor was religion and she went to every workshop that interest her. SHE HAS A WAY WITH CHILDREN AND YOUNG PEOPLE THAT CAUSE ME

TO SHAKE MY HEAD. She can get them to do whatever is necessary. I want to put her in charge of the young adults and children. I don't know one single person who can handle young people like she can.

(Are they at the pastors house who have come back)_

A knock came on the door, it was pastors daughter. She came in smiling, "What are you'll up to." Then she looked around, looking at each of them, "Something is up, I can feel it." The pastor who is her father, explained to her what they had talked about. When he had concluded his talk, she sat there. Twisted around in her chair. Then she looked at Liz, "Are you a part of this resurrection? Liz smiled and bowed her head, saying yes. Then she turned and faced Rev. King, "Count me in. This is going to be a rough ride, but for this purpose I came into this world." They all laugh and shook hands, and without noticing the seven had been chosen. The pastors wife cleared her throat, then she spoke. "I recorder this presentation, so that others may want a copy to listen and remember. I know that most of you were there when

Rev. King made his presentation to the five churches. But you may desire to go over it before the meeting in Seguin, Texas." listen to it tonight." They thanked her for being so thoughtful.

When they arrived in Seguin, all seven will be there

CHAPTER # 11

Meeting of the minds

(It may well be said that often the most dangerous
sin of all is conformity)

A week or two later they arrived in Seguin, Texas. Went to the rooms
that they had reserved. A meeting was called just before they went to
dinner. Rev. King wanted to see who all was there. Later that night
King called the state convention president and informed him that
they were meeting to finalize the plan they had put together. The
President of the state did not seem to be overjoyed, it was almost as
if he did not care. He stood there after he had hung up the phone.
He was disappointed to say the least. He went over to the window
that faced I-10, and watched the cars flying by. He did not like the
mood that he was in; there was still enough time in the day to go
fishing. He had to do something to clear his mind. He had a friend
that lived close by who liked to fish with fishing canes instead of rod
and reel. So he asked everybody if they wanted to go old time fishing
with a fishing pole and line. Most of them thought that it was a good
idea, two or three declined the trip. Then they decided to attend a
drag race only a few miles from where they live.

After breakfast the next morning they met in a private room that
had been reserved for them. Rev. King had the first say, " We have
had a hective month and now all have come down to this. When we

walk out of here we will put the plan into action. I know we said that we would turn the program over to the state, and we are not going back on our word. But I have received information that it will be held up until after the state convention. They do not plan to act on it, and then they will tell us that this is our business, not the state, but they will look over it. By then we will be a year down the road and would have done nothing. We cannot wait, we must not wait, we must move forward if we are to succeed. Is there anyone present that disagrees with my thoughts for success for this District Association." They all agreed. When they left Seguin they would battling Satan for lives and the privilege to strengthen the association.

Liz read the minutes from each meeting and had recorded every get together, even if it was only two or three people. She would give the outcome of each meeting. The group was extremely happy about the presentation that they had made to the five churches.

They were beside themselves to learn from Rev. King that all five churches had agreed to return to the association. Some in the group had heard about the presentation and the things offered in the package, and they wanted to hear about it. But no other churches was contacted, no pastor called. After these five churches, and after this meeting, we will decide what church, and when, and who will be contacting them, no one will influence us to move away from our plan.

Rev. King opened the meeting to chose who would be over the ministry's involvement. Rev. and Sister Hinton was choose to be over the administration of the entire program. He and his wife would work together, they all agreed. Pastor (David Hollman) and his wife would team up together. Bro. Walker and Liz would team up and work together. Bro. Holmes who had written the book that they were going to study and follow, would work alone. He would spend considered time talking to the membership of these churches. He would spend weeks in the field at times, just communicating with the people in different neighborhood. Where ever there is a conflict he would be there. People would learn to respect his opinion.

If he hear something going on in one of these churches during the week. Casual conversation and breakfast at the waffle house would put him in the path of information. . He would then report back to Rev. King and Hinton. He listen for the response of local Church members as to how they felt about what they were hearing, especially the association. He would develop a friendship with some of them to know how they really felt. He wanted to know what they thought about those persons who were over the association. He got an ear full at the barber shop. He had asked the pastors daughter to frequent hair dressers shop for information. She would keep a small recording in her purse to record the conversations. When churches wanted someone to speak from the new group that had just come into power, he would be the one. He was a loner, kind of like an outsider, he would not be known as an insider, but a maverick.

CHAPTER #12

Ministries in waiting

Man responds with his mind. God created man a thinking being., capable of understanding the truth of God's revelation.

Rev. King looked at the group and decided that they would divide the group into subject matters. Each group would visit a church and share two or three of the topics. It was clear to him now, that the entire package could not be shared with each church. The church would investigated before sending a group to share with them. Each group is asked to convince the church they are sharing with, to accept the challenge of returning back to the association. It was clear to most of them that the state were not on their side. They were to stand-by until this group could build a foundation and then they were to dispose of the.

Rev. King got up from his seat and found the same window as before, this time he was looking at Texas Lutheran College, over the tall corn stocks that grew in the field.. Then he said, still looking out the window, We will choose, then he hesitated, turn around and again looked at the group. I have looked carefully at the churches that has fallen away or dismissed. I have looked at the leadership in those churches, and especially where the women seem to have the final say, where pastors are courting women in his church for power. There is another problem; where the deacons stand tall in the church and demand that they are running the church. There is not a church on that list, that does not have some kind of conflict. Where Satan is, and he is every where, there will be conflict.

\I have gotten with SISTER Liz, and as all of you know, on a certain day, and a certain time, I have asked you to pray for a certain thing. I believe that under the guidance of God All Mighty we have brought to you another part of the plan. This plan that we are sharing will be instated into District Association for continued study. If each church can accept three of these concepts and make a commitment to God to practice them. There is no doubt we will be successful.

He hesitated for another moment, "I don't know if we have discussed the issue of same sex marriage. Any church who will allow same sex marriage's, or homosexuals to take leadership roles, or hold an office Will be dismissed from the association. Any pastor who puts a woman in the pulpit, will be called into session; If he continues to do so, will be brought before the counsel for dismissal. The other rules and policy's that have been written into the association will stand. There were some hesitation. Are there any question;--if not, if and when you think of them, call me and let me know. When the State Convention come to order in October I want to make a good solid report. Don't hurry, please don't hurry. Now if your personality does not match one of the churches on your list, don't force it, let me know, we will make some changes.)

Liz came before the group, Walker could not take his eyes from her, then a big smile came over his face. She flashed her eyes toward him and smiled. She began to read off the topics, then she stopped

Rev. and Mrs. King will share these topics:

Financial Responsibility; The association teaching and believing is that we are to give 10% from the top, the gross, and then an offering. This we give in respect to God owning it all. We will not allow need, or circumstances to get in the way. It is totally dependant upon the Lord within his grace and mercy.

Success, Success, Success; The definition for success- "Knowing your purpose in life, growing to meet your maximum potential, and sowing seed that benefit others." When you follow this definition you will never exhaust your capacity to grow toward your potential or run out of opportunities to help others.

\Obedience/ Commitment:` Jesus knew that increase knowledge come through obedience. He saw that learning truths about him would come in time, if only the disciples was willing to obey. One cannot be a learner who has not learned to follow. He knew that development of character would come only through obedience. This was why he was willing to endure patiently many of their human failing as long as they were willing to obey Him.

Rev. Hilton and Wife will share these topics:

Attitude For Belonging: The man, who must stand between God and the people that God has given him to shepherd, must show that he can handle life situations. But most important, how much information does he have to give that can strengthen those who follow his leadership.)

Respect For God. The lack of respect for God brings on consequences and a blockage of a Christian prayer. The word says, But your iniquities have separated you from God; your sins have hidden His face from you., so that he will not hear.)

Discipline Restored: When the church fails to render discipline as God has commanded, the sin of disobedience rests upon the congregation. "My son do not make light of the Lord's discipline, and do not lose heart when he rebukes you, because the Lord disciplines those he loves, and he punishes everyone he accepts as sons."

Effective Leadership: There is no other single attribute in the life of a man who desires to be pastor or deacon which is more important than leadership. Leadership skills can be learned, but leadership that causes people to follow the individual have been with him since birth. People show leadership skills before they have been asked to serve on any committee or ministry. They must show the ability to make sound decisions and solid judgment. They must be able to work through difficult times in pressure situation's.

Dec. Walker and Liz:

Power of Love: God reminds us to love one another, accept one another, serve one another, comfort one another, forgive one another, honor one another, bear one another burden, encourage one another, pray for one another, and be kind to one another. "A new commandment I give you; love one another. As I have loved you, so you must love one another, by this all men will know that you are my disciples, if you love one another.

Power of Discipleship: Let us give a definition of discipleship that you can live with. It developing a personal, lifelong, obedient relationship with Jesus Christ in which he transforms your character into his likeness; changes your values into kingdom values,; and involve you in His mission in the home, the church, and the world. For you to do this you must become like Jesus.

Holding Up The Pastor's Hand: God has set aside two groups of called people to look over His sheep. The pastor is the spiritual leader of the church; he is the one to whom God has given the vision. The pastor must always realize that with the vision comes a plan to accomplish the vision. And with the vision and plan God informs spiritual deacons that he has given the pastor a plan. They may not know what the vision or plan is, but they know that God gave it to this church through the pastor for his people.

Dec. Holmes:

Spiritual Gifts: No person can enter heaven without a spiritual gift. No Christian can have a relationship with Jesus Christ without at least on spiritual gift. No Christian can please God without that believer knowing their spiritual gift or gifts. Without the operational results of one's spiritual gif, A Christian's life will be dull, spiritless, lack of luster and uninspired. And why shouldn't it be, for that person has decided not to obey God in their spiritual gift or gifts.

Reliable Evangelism: This attitude change is the results of a movement in the mind that wake up the physical,sociological, and spiritual energy power in action. Our response to the tremendous awakening power drives our creative energy to unconscious explode into action that we have created ourselves. It is said that if nothing moves, nothing will happen. If the conscious mind never wakes up, there will be no attitude.

Matthew 28:19-20 Gives us the command to do what no other person can do, except another Christian. It takes a Christian to share the gospel.

Pastor of The First Church ☹

Rev. David Hollman)

Faithful Stewardship: The word and concept will be mentioned more than once; that's because believers have developed the habit of missing the meaning of the definition of stewardship. Stewardship is the use of God given resources for accomplishment of God given goals. Practical stewardship for building the district association can be a bitter pill to swallow. There is nothing easy about following the will of God. There is nothing easy about denying one's self from what one love the most. But

if we are to build with God leading our in front there have to be some pain and discomfort. Stewardship is never easy; neither is it too hard for God.

Pastor Of First Church Daughter, bro. Walker, Sis Liz, Bro Holmes.:

Small Group Ministry\: Small group ministry can add four essentials ingredients to the assimilation mix. (1) Sharing. (2) Study. (3) Support, and (4) Service.

The district association who desires to reach out to strong, aggressive leadership must accept the attitude change and the renewed mindset into an area that they most likely is unfamiliar with. This is important because many of the older pastors and deacons are nor familiar with "Small Group Ministries.". Many have no desire to learn, even though it is easy and effective. The church growth studies have found that for a church to assimilate new people effectively it must have an average of seven small groups for every one hundred adult members.

In-Active Drip-Outs: The right of passage by which people

become members of religious communities are well known. The right of passage by which people leave the 'tipping phenomenon' remain unexplored. Church leadership finds in-active-drop-outs to be an interesting subject, but they can't pull the trigger on action.

God is concerned with in-active members that take the time to place their membership with the local church and then walk away. Listen to the word of God and then determine if he is speaking to you. If a man owns a hundred sheep, and one of them wanders away, will he not leave the ninety -nine on the hills and go looking for the one that wanderer off. In the same way your father in heaven is not willing that any of these little ones shall be lost (Matthew 18:12-14)

Conflict Resolution (A) How e understand conflict influences how we approach conflict resolution.

(B) Conflict is an outgrowth of diversity and difference. As such, conflict is not always negative. Conflict can be used to clarify relationships, open up alternative possibilities, and provide opportunities for mutual growth.

(C Conflict are not always limited to battles between interest and desires. Needs, perceptions, power, values and principals, feeling and emotions, and internal conflict are critical ingredients of out relationships, and the conflict that punctuate relationships. Understanding which components Are involved in a particular conflict is essential to resolve the conflict effectively.

The conference was over. .

The last three months have been a whirlwind; a time when more information came rushing into the mind of Rev, King, more than his thought patterns could absorb. He could never tell his core people that he was confused. He was sure that they would lose respect for him, if they thought that he did not know what he was doing. His insides chose not to follow his mind, they wanted to give up. The mind had a friend that would not let the mind give up. A task have been set before him, there were more questions than answers that he knew. He never thought that God had failed him, he just did not know what to do.

CHAPTER 14

At this time the only thing that he had to do, was close the meeting. But something inside of him. Kept him standing. He fumbled around with putting his papers into his bag. Something had been left out and he did not know what it was. It had all been put together, it had all been discussed, and it was all agreed on. They had eight people committed to the program. But still the core was seven and then twelve mature Christian people. Twelve people dedicated to re-building The Cap/Rock District Association.

Rev. King looked over the group, there were no questions. Yet, he seemed to be reluctant to dismiss them to the highway and then back home. Finally he spoke, "A few days ago I was at this church in Dallas, Texas. I was there to hear one of this century best preacher, pastor and teacher. He is a man who is disrespected and not given honor where honor is due. He has an odd personality, maybe not so odd, maybe different; in any case people do not stick with him as a friend. But he had a two page pamphlet that he taught from, it really got my attention! The last thing that I want you to take with you is his teaching on the subject, "Praying For Spiritual Leaders." I have a handout for you."

I wish you would let me share it with you as he shared it with us that bright sunny morning. Let me speak as if God had given it to me to share with you. Many church membership have failed to pray for their pastor, and spiritual leadership. Here is what I want you to do. You have your morning prayer and evening prayer, and sometime a noon prayer. I wish that you would pray twice in the mid-morning and twice during the mid-evening. These prayer will be from two minutes to three minutes in length. You will only pray for

the pastor and leaders. Your first prayer in the middle of the day could be o n boldness of the gospel. God will lead you into what he want you to pray. Your long prayers will be in the morning and evening, but in-between, during the day and during the night when you cannot sleep. You don't have to be concerned with a long prayer, get your hand-out, choose something to pray for, in two or three minutes you can crying out to God on behalf of leadership and will be guided by the spirit of God. They will occure at two and three minutes at a time; they will be powerful prayers, sincere prayers, prayed from the heart, realizing that the prayers will be short one can talk about a specific thing, close his prayer and say Amen.

(LOOK) We must without a doubt bring more worship into the lives of believing leaders of our church. And then our district association. It is clear that we take worship too lightly, and many times on Sunday morning we go through the motions. We refuse to put out body, mind and soul in apposition for God to use us in his service. While sitting in the pews we think more about what is going on in the world, than in the worship service which is going on around us.

We find the same attitude and mind-set on Wednesday night prayer service, Tuesday brotherhood, Thursday night choir practice, Monday night sister hood. Whenever we meet at church, we have learned to fail at the art of worship. He took a deep breath, with the district association we have to learn not to fail God. Obedient to God bring on many area's of success. No Christian should be without his cover of repentance and obedience, and O, Yes, love and faith. The Cap/Rock district association will lead the state and maybe the country in spiritual maturity.

Each member will pray many two or three minute prayers during the day. They will pray about a single thing at each moment of prayer. They will pray about one or two short things; giving thanks at a moment notice of time, Giving praise for a near miss in the car, Give thanks for a beautiful day, share appreciation of God's blessings and promises. Whenever the feeling hits you; that Gods has step into your life and made a difference; pray a two or three minute prayer, it may be less than that. The prayer must sincere and from the heart. It may be that the prayer may be the only time that you have to worship during the day. You see fifteen or twenty minutes a day for worship bring us alive in the program that God has set before us. Allow worship to be the strongest part of your day, for a man cannot praise God and sin at the same time. Worship is the overall total obedience to an all mighty God.

Worship is basically a personal-centered experience. It is a communion between persons, God and man. This encounter awakens powers and transcendence within us. It is reverently "entered into" A life other than one's own. It is transaction—an actual interchange of energy which involves openness on the part of the worshipper. Worship involves the whole man and not the mere segment of his personhood.

Worship is a conscious act in which the worshipper understands God's revelation toward him and in which the worshipper knowingly turns toward God. The worship of God affects the unconscious as well as the conscious Aspect of personality. However, communion with God is not unconscious experience which demands no response on man's part. The gift of faith comes as a conscious understanding of God as he appears in Christ in the midst of historical realities. Our communion with God gains in intensity as we exercise conscious faith in him. Christian worship is man's loving response in personal faith to God's personal revelation of himself with God in Christ. In essence, is man's communion with God in Christ,

this conscious relationship being affected by the Holy Spirit in the Spirit of the worshipper. Here lies the foundation of our maturity, it is worship.

PRAYING FOR SPIRITUAL LEADERS.

A 10-Day Intercessory Prayer Guide.

I would like to encourage you to read this, copy it, make it a part of your life. Each one of us probably look at someone as our pastor, our spiritual mentor, and/or have a special burden for those who are ministering in other parts of the world. Why not be a fervent intercessor for them?

\Encourage others to support your pastor. Give respect, trust, and above all else become a prayer supporter. You could use this guide as you pray through the list over and over again. And upheld these specific items in prayer for missionaries and others in the ministry. These are good things to pray for one another as well. (Dr.. Edward Watke Jr.--Revival in the House Ministries, www.watke. org-Augusta, B.A,)

Here we are going to look at some suggestion that the pastor made in his sermon. He labored Hard for the prayer from membership to leadership, especially pastors and deacons: I have never heard a pastor desiring the prayers of his membership as this preacher did. I join him in asking each of you to pray for our core group. We have no idea what lie ahead of us. There will be times that it seem as if I am not with you, not on your side, not doing enough, not standing up for the direction of the association. All ways remember that we have put this program together, we have sweated, we have prayed, and we have fought, and now here we are confronted with people we thought were friends. You are going to see a different kind of preacher, a different kind of deacon, a different kind missionary sister, your brotherhood presidents will go against you to favor their pastor. Please remember as you go through this creative plan for success that God is on your side. Do not take the prayer of spiritual leaders lightly.

Some of your prayers will be with tears, some with sweat, some with trembling lips, but let not doubt or fear enter your mind. If it does call on God to deliver you, because it is of Satan.

Let us first look at the suggestions. You can modify any part of this plan, but this is the way that he gave it to us. I just wish that you could have been there and saw the driving attitude that he had. He was almost pleading, then again, maybe there is something that God have showed him that requires this kind of meditation. Maybe God has shown him something in scripture, that we missed, that lingers ahead of us, that he can hear with his spiritual ear. By listening to him, you would think that Jesus have prepared to leave heaven to move toward earth. Then again maybe we all should think that way, because the time we have left is short. If we listen carefully, those who walk with God can hear him pleading with us that His son will be to get the church soon.

>   *. Pray for pastors, missionaries and ministerial staff is one of the most important endeavors in which believers can participate. (Col. 4:2) 1Thess. 5:2)

>   *. Specific, biblical prayers are so very important and the greatest gift you can give to your pastor and all the missionaries for whom you should pray.

>   *. Using this guide alone, or with your family or spouse, or with a small group at church.. Above all take time to pray and praise God for these servants. (Phil. 4:8; Eph. 5:18-21)

>   *. Prepare your own hearts by confessing your sin (Psa. 51:2 32:1-5; 1 John 1:7=9 consider intercession one of the greatest blessings you can bestow on others.

>   *. While most of this is aimed at prayer for pastors- -all of these points apple to those who serve in other lands as missionaries, for national workers, for deacons, for all those who serve in the local church.

DAY ONE:

>   "And for me, that utterance may be given unto me, that I may open my mouth boldly, to make known the mystery of the gospel." (Eph.6:19)

>   *Pray for boldness in the preaching and teaching of the word of God.

*Pray for your pastor to be more interesting in pleasing the Heavenly Father than men.

*Pray that he may experience the power of the Holy Spirit in his preaching.

DAY TWO.

"Study to shew thyself approved unto God, a workman that needeth not to be ashamed, rightly divided the word of truth." (11 Tim.2:15)

* Pray for your pastor to spend much time in the word, gaining wisdom and approval from God.

* Pray for his discernment to grow as he diligently applies himself to accurately handle the word of God, that he might share the whole counsel of God.

* Pray for him to be a good bible teacher (as well as preacher) and that church members will also be encouraged to study the word.

* Pray for your pastor as he prepares his sermons that only the word of God may be revealed, that self does not enter in, but he would be led of the Spirit.

DAY THREE.

"Give therefore thy servant ding heart to judge they people, that I may discern between good and bad:

for who is able to judge this day so great a people?"(1 King 3:9)

* Pray for him to lead the people with godly direction and sensitivity that only the Holy Spirit can give.

*Pray that he may offer guidance to church leadership that may bring unity and share vision and passion.

* Pray for wisdom to be given to your pastor in building a strong ministry team.

DAY FOUR.

"... ... as it is written, how beautiful are the feet of them that preach the gospel of peace and bring glad tiding of good things." (Rom. 10:15)

* Pray for your pastor to be a soul winner, that as he leads souls to Christ he will also teach others to lead souls to the savior. Pray for the church to have evangelistic zeal.

* Pray for the pastor to have vision, to have expectation, and to look for open doors.

*Pray for yours to be a church that focus on bringing the lost to saving grace.

* pray for the pastor to lead the church to sacrificially support a worldwide missionary endeavor.

----

k1

DAY FIVE.

> "Let your speech be always with grace, seasoned with salt, that ye may know how ye ought to answer every man." (Col. 4:6)

> * Pray for your pastor to have the grace to know how to respond to complaints from church members. That he may be open, loving, and gracious in his dealings with others.

> * Pray for him to be found blameless and innocent and to have favor with those he services.

> * Pray for him to be a peacemaker and one who brings reconciliation.

DAY SIX.

> "Where there is no counsel, the people fall; but in the multitude of counselors there is safety." (Prov. 11:14)

> * Pray for your pastor and the other spiritual leaders of the congregation that they would pray and seek wise counsel before making decisions. And they they lead with unity.

* Pray for clear guidance from your pastor through biblical insight for church growth plans and policy.

* Pray for him to be trusted and followed as the under shepherd of your congregation.

DAY SEVEN.

"If any of you lack wisdom, let him ask of God, that giveth to all men liberally, and upbraided not; and it shall be given him." (James 1:5)

*Pray for your pastor to have a spirit of humility and to willingly ask God for wisdom in leading the church body.

* Pray for your pastor to regularly teach by example with total dependency upon God. That he might know the will of God and lead the flock in God's will and plan.

* Pray most of all that your pastor, and you, will seek God's glory first." (Eph. 1:12; Matt.6:33.)

DAY EIGHT.

"And he spake a parable unto them to this end, that me ought to always pray and not to faint." (Luke 18:1)

*Pray for your pastor, that above everything else, he will be a man of prayer who also teaches others to pray. That he will know what it means to be importunate in prayer.

* Pray for the steadfast spirit within your pastor that he will not lose heart.

* Pray that your pastor will lead the congregation to be known as a praying church. That he will be a prayer warrior for missionaries and prompt the people toward intercession.

DAY NINE.

"He that hath my commandments, and keepeth them, he it is that loveth me: and he that loveth me shall be loved of my father, and I will love him ..." ..." (John 14:21) (152)

* Pray for your pastor to be an obedient servant of Jesus who leads the church to obey.

* Pray for your pastor to enjoy sweet fellowship with the Lord, loved by the father. (John 14:21-23)

* Pray that a spirit of obedience to Christ (to the word) may permeate pastor and people.

DAY TEN.

"... ... he might be a vessel unto honor, sanctified, meet for the master's use." (11Tim.2:21)

* Pray for his family, his children and spouse to be godly, vessels unto honor.

* Pray for his wife to be the helpmate God intended her to be, with obedient children.

*Pray for pastor and family to take time to nurture their relationship with each other. To take time off when needed, to know the joy of ministry together, for God's glory.

Rev. King made sure that each person had a copy of the handout. He took a deep breath. "Make sure you have every thing that you came with and then a few others." He then asked Rev. Hinton to close out in prayer. Rev. Hinton stood, opened his bible to (2Chronicles 7:14NIV) Then he read slowly and with power, " If my people, who are called by my name, will humble themselves and pray and seek my face and turn from their wicked ways, then will I hear from heaven and will forgive their sin and will heal their land" When he had read the scripture, he dropped his head and prayed. Rev. King watched them file out of the meeting room. When the last person had left the room, he took a deep breath and thanked God for the message.

While he stood there he thought about the time when Jesus choose his twelve disciples. A small smile crossed his face, a smile a smile that he now had something to measure the selection of his followers. Slowly he sat back into his seat, thinking about the time that Jesus had to make this same decision. He folded his arms tightly around his body, and let the Holy Spirit speak to him. The spirit shared with him that at the time of the selection of the twelve; that Jesus had come to a very important moment in his life and work. He had emerged with his message; He had gone through out the country teaching and healing.

First, he had to find a way of making his message permanent if anything happen to him, and that something would happen he did not doubt. Second, he had to fine some way of disseminating his message, and in an age when there was no such thing as a printed book or newspaper, no way of reaching large number of people at one time, that was no easy task.

There was only one way to solve these pending problems; he had to choose certain men on whose hearts and lives he could write his message and who would go out from his presence to carry this message abroad.

It significant that CHRISTIANITY BEGAN WITH A GROUP. The Christian faith is something which from the beginning had to be discovered and lived out in a fellowship. The whole essence of the way of the Pharisee was that it separated men from their followers; the very name Pharisee means separated one; the whole essence of Christianity was that it bound men to their fellows and for each other.

When you look at the men that Jesus chose, they had no special qualifications at all. They were not wealthy; they had no special social position; they had no special education; they were not trained theologians; They were no high ranking churchmen. They were ordinary men. But they had two special qualification. First, they had felt the magnetic attraction of Jesus. There were something about him that made them wish to take him as their master., And, second, they had the courage to show that they were on his side.. Make no mistake, that did require courage.

CHAPTER #13

Call to share the message

"May the God of peace himself sanctify you wholly;
and may your spirit and soul and body be kept
sound and blameless." (1 Thess. 5:23)

Jesus called them to him for two purposes. First, he called them
to be with him. He called them to be his steady and consistent
companions. Others may come and go; the crowd might be there
one day and away the next; others may be fluctuating and spasmodic
in their attachment to him, but these twelve were to identify their
lives with his life and live with him all the time. Second, he called
them to send them out. He wanted them to be his reprehensive. He
wanted them to tell others about him. They themselves had been
won in order to win others.

For this task Jesus equipped them with two things. First, he gave
them a message. They were to be his heralds. A wise man said that no
one has the right to be a teacher unless he has a teacher of his own to
offer, or the teacher of another that with all the passion of his heart
he wishes to propagate. Men will always listen to the man with a
message.. Jesus gave these friends of his something to say. Second he
gave them a power, they were also to cast out demons. Because they
companied with him something of his power was on their lives."
Rev. King whispered to himself, "Cast out demons". He did not have

the slightest idea how to cast out a demon. Yet, he knew it would be a part of his administration. Just thinking about the task ahead, of things that he knew about and things that God would show him; brought on a cold sweat, and a temporary nervous condition. (154)

He finally was able to walk to the door, standing on his own two feet. He stood at the door for a small while, looking back into an empty room. Then he realizing that there was something that he had forgotten. Finally it hit him, The Lords Supper. It was too late to bring them back, but at the next meeting he will share with them the importance of the Lord Supper. He will remind them that they could sleep because of un-worthly living, and the refusal to repent of their sins. He also knew that being, Born Again, was not clear in many people's mind. He will make it clear and to the point.

The question of women in the pulpit? This association would not have women in the pulpit. It was his belief that the bible taught that the pulpit was designed for men, and that women were not to be over men. The bible has taught this fact throughout the bible and have implied it in other ways. It does not feel natural for them to be in any other place except on the floor. Pastors teaching men how to be deacons and leaders. Many of our local pastors have failed to teach men what their responsibility is. Yes, men are harder to learn than women, a woman will step out into something that she does not know anything about, if her pastor says that she can do it, she will do it.

Rev. King noticed that there were two pastors who had come into the meeting about an hour ago. He had assumed that they were invited by members of the group, so until now he did not say anything. But mentally he noticed that they seem to be against everything that he said. They did not say anything to him, but they would talk out loud and influence his own people. At the close of the meeting he invited the two pastors for lunch at Bill Collins bar-be-cue. They gladly accepted the invertation, looking at each other grinning as if they had won an argument.

Soon after they had ordered their lunch, the two pastors looked at each other and bowed their heads. One pastor inquired about the district association, an area that was out of his jurisdiction. It angered Rev. King a little, but he remain calm. It was not long before he saw what they were after, they wanted to become movers and shakers in the national convention. They were young and because they sang well and could hoop with the best of them that they could move to the top quickly by becoming head of a department of the state convention. They though that going through the district association, which was limping alone on one leg; they and their large church could control the district, and the state would have to deal with them. The two of them with their church's and the outside influence of ungodly people who only cared about themselves; would form a heartless position that would in time make one of them president and the other dean of the national convention.

They went on to tell him that they had the two best choirs in the state of Texas. They tried to convince Rev. King that they were two best preachers in the state of Texas. They assured him that they were preachers of power and influence. They compared themselves with Dr. C.B.T. Smith and Dr. Fabian K. Jacko. They bragged about how they have people jumping benches, crying and screaming. There were some women who wanted to leave their husbands for them even though they had wives. They went on to say that they did not have to leave their husbands, we are there to serve.

Rev. King could take it no more. His street temper rose, but he was calmed down when he looked under the table and saw that each of them had weapons. They reminded him that they were going to be running things through him. It was then that the cursing and name calling escalated above the conversation in the restaurant. A Godly couple sitting next to them came over quickly and tried to calm them down. Rev. King cooled down and soon apologized to all who was in hearing distant. But only the entrance of the police did the pastors quiet down. They showed the police officers that they had a licene to carry a weapon.. The police asked the two pastors to come outside, it appeared that they all knew each other. Finally the police asked Rev. King if he would leave. The owner would perfer for them to leave. Immediately, he got up and went to his car. The police Sgt. Asked one of the patrol drivers to follow him to 35 North. As King. was getting into his car, one of the pastors cursed him, "We don't need you anymore. You are too stupid to be alive."

Rev. King was a little shaken, he had not expected them to have guns, and certainly did not expect them to pull them on him in a public place. They were so calm with the deadly pulling of death in a public place. He knew without a doubt that they would kill him and would have the law to back them up. Then he said to himself, "No I don't believe that. I must be going out of my mind. He tried to reason with himself, how in the world did he get into this mess. He thanked God that the godly people interrupted before he had gotten to his gun. The Christian spirit went beyond the clouds and did not show itself until he was comfortably on 35 North.

When he had calmed down outside and inside; the smooth road toward Dallas was enjoyable. His mind went over to more positive things. He thought about leadership. They did not want these kind of people that he had just left in the convention. Then he thought, for a while he was there with that group and if they had not gotten to their guns first, he would have had his. Only God knows what would have happen. He saw then that there were changes that he would have to make if he was to be successful. Changers, Yes, changes within himself and for a while it frighten him. He had not intended to make changes, but to operate within change.

He sat his speed control on seventy five and relaxed. He thought about leadership: There is no other single attribute in the life of a man who desires to be a leader, deacon or pastor which is more important than leadership. Leadership skills can be learned, but leadership that cause people to follow the individual has been with him since birth. People show leadership skills before they have been asked to serve on any committee or ministry. They must show the ability to sound decisions and sound judgment. They must be able to work through difficult times in pressure situations. This man must be able to keep standing even though he is knocked down. He may not be aware of it himself, but other people see leadership ability in every day activity. The true measure of leadership is influence, nothing more and nothing else. He knew that he could not keep on making mistakes like what just happen.

He was thinking about the Christians first priority? The love of God. The desire for obedience. Personnel commitment to God. The person who desires to be moderator must appeal to the membership because of his love for God and His people. He cannot find the depth of God's love, if Jesus Christ does not abide in him. When Jesus abide in us, and we in him,, it bring the assurance of eternal life, For the love of God flows through his body, soul and spirit. His desire to love God's people and to help strengthen them in their ministry shows how much he cares. Long before a man go on trial or is looked toward filling a leadership role, the church should see leadership ability, and positive traits that they admire in the potential leader. His ability to teach the word of God and rightly divide the word for understanding and application is essential.

The moderator had just got outside of Georgetown when his phone rang. Without trying to see who the caller was he answerer it. The caller was the pastor of one of the five churches that had agreed to come aboard. He had a somewhat unique problem. His wife of 15 years had confronted him about his relationship with one of the young women in their congregation. He told Rev. King that at first he had denied the allegations, that was before he knew that she had hired an investigator to take pictures and record the date's of his activity. According to him, she did not try to conceal the pictures and wait on a court date to reveal them. She came out and laid the entire situation on the table. After he had told her that there were no love involved, he just made a mistake. Then he ended his comments with, It was a mistake that I wanted to make.

She told him that she would not leave him as long as he was pastor of a church. But she wanted him to go back to the church that he received his liciens and the church that ordained, and sent him out to share in leadership. She wanted that church to disown him and disgrace him. She wanted people to look down on him with contempt. Rev. King asked him if this was the first time that he had courted a woman in his church. The answer, was no. He told Rev. King he had a couple of kids in his congregation that was not born to his wife. Rev. thought for a moment. He knew that this sticky situation were not going away. The wife is hurt because the women talks about her when they think that she is not listening. When the two women who are kind of friends, who do some things together have lately made a habit of laughing at women when they take their man away from them. Or gets the man's attention with a little sex on the side. They talk about how good he is in bed, and the other things that he does that blow their minds. They always get a big laugh out of it, then walk off shaking their back side. Rev. King. knew the situation and he knew how the wife felt.. When the pastor first started to go with these two women, he would come home, whip his wife and throw her out of the house.

She would always come back, but even then he did not care if she came back or not.

He knew that the church could or would not remove any of the qualifications that they had restored upon him. He is a preacher, he is a preacher for life. But he understood the wife had come to a breaking point, for her there had to be some kind of revenge. The wife wanted to maintain her Christian life. She wanted people to respect her. She had tried a couple of the deacons, but that did not work out. He knew that she was one miserable woman. She had gotten to the point that she would do anything to rob him of his power. She had to see him hurt, she had to see him miserable, she wanted to see him broke and out of a job. She wanted to see him homeless and under the bridge.

Rev. King asked the pastor again. Did you knowingly sin against these women sexually. Did you tell them anything to force or trick them into your bed. The pastor said that he told the both of them separate, how they will be helping the pastor by having sex with him, that will keep him fresh. He said that he told them they will be blessed and find favor with God by helping His anointed one. They agreed and was happy to help the pastor out. I told them that my wife was fridget and cold and did not want to have sex. Matter of fact I told them my wife did not want me to sleep with her at nights. "Pastor," he said, "some of all of this is true at one time then the other, I did not totally lie to them. Matter of fact they wanted an excuse to lay with this dark handsome man. We all together done what we wanted to do and enjoyed the experience. Pastor King asked him if there were any other women in the church that he had been to bed with. He admitted that he tried quite a few of them until he found what he wanted.

Rev. King hesitated for a few minutes, reminding the young man that he was still on the phone. Finally he said. "Pastor did you know that you were sinning, that you were unfaithful to God, that you were breaking your covenant agreement with your wife." There were another long silence, "Yes I knew that I was wrong, but I also knew that God would forgive me, and it would not interfere with my trip to the kingdom." Rev. King started to say something, but then he stopped. Finally he asked the young pastor, "What would have happen to you if you had dies during the time you were having a good time." Then he said, "My earlier salvation was never disconnected, I was saved then and I'm saved now. That is what I have been told and I believe it.

Pastor King pulled his car over to a road side park near Temple, Texas. He told the young pastor not to leave home he would call him back. He wanted to make sure that as his moderator he would give him the best information that he could give. He reached over into his satchel and retrieved a book called, "The Doctrine and Administration of the Church by PAUL R. Jackson. He turned to page 144, 4th paragraph. "Ordination by the church does not impart to the man any divine authority or power. It is the recognition by the church of the fact that it believes that God has called and ordained the man as His servant. The ordination by the church constitute a commendation of the man for public leadership and ministry.

Ordination is not necessarily perpetual. It is valid only as long as the man adhers to the doctrine and conduct which were the basis for his ordination.

If he become unsound in doctrine, moral conduct or other areas, the church of which he is then a member may, and should, rescind the ordination, regardless of who granted it. Only the church which a person is a member can exercise discipline. Therefore, a church should not drop a person from membership upon the request of that person if discipline should be exercised. The church has no jurisdiction after the membership has been terminated." "Your wife have not come to me as her moderator, if and when she does, I will read the word and pray to God for guidance.

Another silence settled in between them, then finally, "Moderator King, what you are saying, you are going to take her side. You must have forgotten that pastors and men stand up for each other. I know that I was wrong, we have all be wrong, and sinned, we have been unfaithful not one time but many times. I am no worse than any other preacher who stands in the pulpit and share the word. I want you to know that the church that ordained and licensed me is not in your district. King thought to himself, if the wife come to me about the things that had happen over the last ten years, I will have to use this case, this problem, this mistake-no it wasn't a mistake. What he wanted was against God will for pastors and he did it any way. He knew it was wrong, before his wife, the women that he sin with and most of all against God. Even when God tried to help him, he disregarded God help. 1 Corinthians 10:13 NIV. "No temptation has seized you except what is common to man. And God is faithful, he will not let you be tempted beyond what you can bear. But when you are tempted, He will also provide a way out. So that you can stand up under it." Rev. King became so frustrated that he told the pastor that he would call him when he got back to Dallas.

The moderator was getting a taste of what it was being in

the position that lie ahead of him. He got our of the car and sat back on the front left wheel covering. The truck that went by said, HAGWOOD TRANSPORTATION, Dallas, Texas. With all the trucks passing him one way or the other, this was the first one he notices. He looked down the road both ways, cars and trucks passing and they did not pay him any attention. He walked over to the water fountain and got him a drink of water. A cute little girl approximately eight months old kept watching him. When he looked at her, she never smiled. He looked around one of the persons standing there taking pictures and looked at the little girl and she broke out into a laugh and hid her face. It put a smile on his face and brought joy to his heart. He went back to his car, but he was not ready to leave. He knew that there had to be punishment, but it sadden him to discipline a pastor.

He looked down the road toward Dallas, and the distant automatic got shorter. He thought then that maybe he should have bought his wife. Maybe they could get into a good argument about nothing. But the word conduct and discipline and retribution kept blowing wind into his mind. Finally he sat back into the car, but he did not turn on the key. He now wondered what was all that about over the last two months. He wanted to doubt his trip to the second heaven, but he thought about what God had said to him and Joshua at different times. He thought about how mature saved people glorify the savior. He felt a little sick of the stomach and embarrassed when he thought about the things that passed through his mind.

His thoughts went back to before his time, a time that he heard about when he was a kid. There were this preacher call Rector, one called Byrd, one Wilkerson and then there was Hotterman. He had heard about them over the years. His great grand father had left him a sermon that Rector had preached in the association out side of Seguin, back in the early fifties. He looked in his satchel and when he could not find it; he opened the trunk of his car, looked in a box that been tied up with twine, and there it was. He sat back in his car and began to read.

"The glorifying of God is the highest pinnacle of human privilege and responsibility, As men we are not likely to consider it so. Things which affect our destiny or our comfort and happiness too often take precedence in our thinking. But the Bible is emphatic on this subject, that is glorify the savior.

Our conduct is to be governed by a desire to Glorify God. What? Know yea not that your body is the temple of the Holy Ghost which is in you, which Ye have of God, and you are not your own? For you are bought with a price: Therefore glorify God in your body, and in your spirit, which is God's (1 Cor. 6:19, 20.) Our actions are not to be governed by what we think is to our best advantage, but by a responsibility to act for God's glory. Whether therefore ye eat, or drink,, or whatsoever you do, do all to the glory of God. Many problems in the business and social life of Christians would be quickly settled by this principal. Many professed Christians argue about smoking, theaters, worldly companions and other similar things. They give this feeble defense: I can't see anything wrong with it. That is negative and wholly inadequate. Is there anything right about it? Will the things under consideration glorify God? That must be the basis of decision for the spiritual man.

Our confession of Christ and His worthiness should bring glory to him constantly. This is God's will for all ages, including the present.

We are to acknowledge His authority over us in our preaching, prayer, singing and in all of our attitudes. We are to preach not ourselves, but Christ Jesus out Lord.

Our testimony should give glory to the savior as we confess Him before men. All before whom we live should be made conscious of His great power. They should be made to realize. That as Christians we are what we are by the grace of God. The very purpose of the church existence are to teach us that we should be to the praise of his glory."

Rev. King thought for a moment. He looked out toward the freeway where cars were passing in rapid sections. Not a one of them looked in his direction. He stood there drenched in one of the most beautiful days of his life. It was one of those days that seem too good to be true. Every thing that stood before him occupied its space in God's order. It was kind to the tough and the feel of the soft wind blowing into his face. Yet, today's situation set in and he had to face reality. He could not understand why God was snatching him around. One moment he would face him with the best that he has to offer humans; and then snatch him into a struggling world of misunderstanding.. He looked back at the papers and thought that he could do without this, but he read on anyway. He could just imagine Rev. Rector leaning upon the pulpit with both elbows. He wanted the association to get what he was about to say. He was silence for a brief while as he looked down toward the first seats before him. Then he straighten up and with a voice of sincerity, he spoke from his heart.

With the falling away of God's people from his divine purpose; with the failure to repent of un-repented sins due to the disobedience of God's word; with the groaning disrespect of the Sanctuary of God, God himself, His son and the Holy Spirit, brings to the local church a warning; especially those who are enjoying the bigness and the emotional excitement of their worship../ A church which is crowded with people and which is a hive of energy is not necessary a real church. It is possible for a church to be crowded because its people come to be entertained instead of instructed, and to be soothed instead of confronted with the fact of sin and the offer of salvation; it may be a highly successful Christian club rather that a real Christian congregation.

He slowly put the papers back in the box and re-rapped the contents for safe keeping. He asked himself, how in the world did he get into this situation. It did not matter, he had been chosen by God, to lead this people before him. Then he began to ask himself questions about how a pastor could get so far off track. It was like silence and dumbness clashed together in the middle of his mind. He had no proof that the young preacher/pastor was saved in the first place. The church that ordained and license him took his word for his salvation. They truly did not ask God to lead them in knowing that he was saved. He thought back over the years that he knew the young man. All of these years he was kind of light and not sound around the edges. He was always talking about what other people had said. Or what this book and that book said, seldom did he ever say what God had said.

He agreed with the establishment that a man having sex outside the family would not lead him to hell. A sin, yes, wrong, yes, destroys a marriage, Yes, Interfere with a man's relationship with his father, Yes. But God will forgive him and through God's grace and mercy he will finish his life in heaven.

He opened the door and sat quietly in his car, thinking about what he should do. As he sat there some thoughts ran across his mind. He thought that one of the most neglected doctrines of the word of God is church discipline. It is encouraging to learn from our missionaries that our national churches in other land are more faithful to these scriptures teaching than are most of our churches in the homeland.

Neglect of church discipline is in line with the general trend in our current social and educational development. The lack of adequate authority and discipline in homes, schools, governments and churches can certainly be blamed as a major factor in the lawlessness and delinquency on every hand. Bible-believing churches ought not to be a part of this worldly philosophy. The success of the apostates in capturing the organizations and church of the great denomination is due largely to the failure of the past generation in our churches to judge and remove unbelievers instead of allowing them to multiply and gain control. We need to learn from their costly lesson the urgency of dealing with sin. To fail to do so not only allows it to become entrenched, it grieves the Holy Spirit and thus rob us of his power and enabling to discern and resist sin. May the Lord revive within us willingness to obey His Word in this responsibility of discipline.

You can't think about discipline without thinking about forgiveness. Forgiveness to those who repent and confess is a basic law of the Word. He thought about the Lords Word in Luke 17:3-4. Little wonder, in the light of our own haughty, unforgiving hearts, the next words of his disciples were, "increase your faith." The absolute standard of forgiveness is set before us in Eph. 4:32 "And be ye kind one to another, tenderhearted, forgiving one another, even as God for Christ's sake hath forgiven you." His forgiveness to us was not of the sort, "I shall forgive, but I can never forget," He forgave us fully, freely and finally. On the other hand he laid down restraints, "Them that sin rebuke before all, that others also may fear." 1 Timothy 5:20. He said in Heb.10:32 " It is a fearful thing to fall into the hands of the living God." In another place, :For whom the Lord loveth he chasteneth, that is found somewhere in the book of Hebrews.

Rev. King wrestled with the word of God, not that he did not believe. He had a conflict because the pastor was a kind of friend of his. He wanted to give the young man ever opportunity to straighten himself up.. But then the church has a solemn responsibility to restrain sin by proper discipline. If we do nor exercise the judgment, the Lord will. "For if we would judge ourselves, we should not be judged. But when we are judged, we are chastened of the Lord, that we should not be condemned with the world"

(1 Cor. 11:31-32.)

Rev. King sat there in his car for a moment. He did not know what to think. Every direction that his mind went in, there were a problem, there were a conflict between he and his friend. He now wondered if he could have done something when he heard the rumors of the pastors adultery ways. When other preachers were bragging about this pastor had two good looking women with bodies. They applauded him for not having to pay the women, it was a free ride. Some of the church women hung their heads in sorrow and unbelief, that their pastor would stoup to this level of living. But some thought that it was cute, they wish they could be there.. He tried to find another position in his car that he could sit in. When he turned his face toward the passengers side, he saw his bible., He looked at it for a moment, then picked it up and turned to (Matthew 18:2 NIV) "He called a little child and had him stand among them. And he said: "I tell you the truth, unless you change and become like little children, you will never enter into the kingdom of heaven. Therefore, whoever humbles himself like this child is the greatest in the kingdom of heaven. And whoever welcomes a little child like this in my name welcome me. But if anyone cause one of these little one who believe in me to din, it would be better for him to have a large millstone hung around his neck and be drowned in the depth of the sea." He thought to himself, Woe to the man through who they come.

He knew that he was putting too much time into a situation that had already played itself out on the stage of life. The sin had been committed, the wrong done in four places, himself, his wife and the two young women. But then there were the two children, which is the consequence of this man's sin. For the rest of his life they will look back at him, they will love him, jump up into his arms and call him daddy. The wife will stand a far off and look upon them with disgust knowing that she has been cheated out of her covenant agreement with her husband. Even if they stay together, their marriage, relationship will never be the same again. Rev. King knew that he has to help this young man and then protect the church, and above all do the will of God. He closed his bible and decided to take a nap.

He was a little tired, the meeting had been a little distressful. There were parts of the puzzle that were bland, no names had been inserted.

When he dropped off to sleep, he was in an environment of tall cedar trees that surrounded him. The rain had fallen through many tall trees before resting on the leaves of the flowers that had their roots into the ground. The rain and mist seem to have fallen on leaves of all kind. The water rested on them only for a little while then fell to the ground. Only a few small puddles of water stood to look up to the sky. The sky was hard to see for the tree limbs with leaves. In between a group of trees was a lighted area and he saw Jesus Christ as though he was about to walk past the opening in the trees; He looked back toward Rev. King with a pleasant look on his face. It was plain that he was on his way to his father, and He took time to look upon his servant who had been assigned a great responsibility. And then he was gone.

CHAPTER #14

Are you willing to pay the price?

(God appears to man as HOLY SPIRIT. The Holy
Spirit is personal and not merely an atmosphere. In
man's worship God is present as the manifestation
of the father and of the Son.)

Rev. King looked around him and there had not been any rain for
months. But he felt clear about his responsibility. If the wife came
to him and requested that her husband license and ordination be
withdrawn from him, he would have to respond. Not only because
the wife requested it. But his action was damaging to the church.
No sooner had he thought about what to do his phone rang. It was
his wife telling him that Barkley's wife was steaming. Barkley is the
wife of the preacher with the problem. She had gone to the church
and they had said that they could do nothing about the situation.
She informed him that as soon as he arrives back in Dallas, she
wanted a conference with him. She went on to say that the wife
want his ordination and license rescinded. They talked for a while
and then hung up. He knew then that if she came to him, he would
have to act.

He dialed the chairman of the board. When he asked the
chairman about the acquaintance (sp). The chairman admitted;
that it was more than a rumor. All most every person in the church

knew about it, even some of the small ones knew. Because they had heard these women brag about the fact that their child was his children half sister and brothers. He went on to tell Rev. King that their hands are tied, because when they built the new building, it was built on his property. The church was unaware that he had purchased the property next to the church. He now owned the church and we cannot get rid of him. Rev. King ask (Inquired of the) the chairman if he would put together a nomination committee would he serve on it to remove the license and ordination from Rev. Barkley. The chairman said he would.

Rev. King got out of his car walked over and talked to a trucker for about twenty minutes and then he returned to car. While he was standing next to his car a little 1 year old girl dressed in all her curls came by and spoke to him. He nodded, she went a few more step and stopped, "Are you feeling o.k.. mister, you don't look good, I'm going to get you a drink of water. My mommy is a nurse, she will come an help you" When the lady returned with her daughter it was one of the young women that Rev. Barkley had been with, or was still having an affair with. She rushed up to him to assist, but he told her that he was all right. Then she asked him why was he looking at her in such a peculiar way. He asked her if she knew Rev. Stanley Barkley? She looked at kind of strangely, "Who are you, what do you want." He went on to tell her who he was and what his position was as the moderator. He kept looking at the little girl and he wanted to know if she and Barkley were relatives. When she wanted to know why, he informed her that there were a resemble.

She smiled at him, "This is his daughter, she has a lot of his ways" Rev. King stood there for a while in shock, then she and the little girl turned and walked away. The little girl was saying by--by--by as she walked away from the moderator. It was set, he had to move. This would be an opportunity to get the attention of the district, state and national.

He got back in his car, reached into his satchel and pulled out a secretary pad. He sketched out a form for the assembly of the nomination committee to rescind the ordination and license of Pastor Stanley E. Barkley.

\ CALL TO RECEND THE ORDINATION AND LICENSES:

The--Baptist Church of
---to the
---Baptist Church of
\--

Dear Brothers:

You are requested to send your pastor and two brothers to sit
\with us in council on--------in------------------to consider
\the advisability of setting aside to the gospel ministry our brother
\----------------------------who is a member of our church. The council
Will convene at --------------------------P.M.
If the council acts favorably, the ordination service for to rescind of the ordination and license will be held---
\done by order and in behalf of the church.
\City--
\Date--
\---Church Clerk.

The following churches and individuals are invited:
\

He looked at the form and regret that anything in this world could come to this. He called the secretary of the district association; and asked her to call all of the churches in the district including the one's that they are looking forward to bringing them back into the fold. He wanted to have the meeting before the resceinding of the license and ordination of a local pastor. He knew that he needed time to talk about this action, because most people in the district felt as if once you were license and, or, There were no doubt that this was not going to be a friendly issue, license and ordained, it would hold for life. But to set a popular brother aside because of reason-=-----. He knew that he would have to have his cap on tight. He would have to have evidence, and he believed that he could get that from the women, his wife and some of the women at the hair dressing shop.

With the meeting set as soon as the pastors could be notified. Bringing the brother before the council was a matter of asking the pastors and deacons of the churches invited. He knew that he had to solve this problem as soon as possible.(The preachers in the district would be behind the moderator if he did not make some moves that would surprise everybody.) He had to find a loop hole that would give him an out, to keep from taking his license. And yet it must seem like he wanted to take away his ordination. He needed for this to show his strength and leadership skills. This was a tough case to confront the church and the district. All eyes were looking to see what would happen. Not only in Texas, but all across the country people were watching to see what would be the outcome. The Baptist Church's throughout the country had four national Baptist Conventions. The head of each convention had agreed to meet in a one day session to see what decision they thought would be best for all concern. Tomorrow, on short notice, they had agreed to meet in Chicago Ill. And they had asked a few leading pastors in that area if they would attend. All who was notified agreed to come. Their meeting would not help Rev. King to make his decision. They would not say a word until after Rev. King had made his decision)

The older members wanted his papers to be rescinded; they did not think that he was fit to stand in the pulpit. They did not think that he was worthy to carry the name preacher, Dr. or, pastor; he should not be allowed to be near the pulpit, he should be banned for life from being a deacon or preacher. The more mature members were on her side, but the young people was leaning toward the young preacher. How many people the pastors wife had on her side could be a problem. Most of the young people would not come to an ordination counsel meeting. She would have no problem getting the senior people to come on a Saturday morning at 10.00 A.M. The look in her eyes, as he remembered her, she would not stop until he was disgraced. She wanted him run out of the church.

What she had in her favor, he did not detest the divorce. Living with her had been a sore spot for him the last five years. It wasn't anything that she had done, but he had outgrown her. He no longer wanted her for any reason, but he could not afford to divorce her, it would look bad for the pulpit. He had thought about quit preaching all together, but he did not want to work and the church paid him a good salary with benefits. Rev. King knew what decision that he had to make, but he did not know how to make this decision that most likely would set president for the Baptist Church through out the country.

A thought struck him as he drove toward Dallas. There is a flaw in the city wide brotherhood that had to be cleaned up. They had drawn up a litney of who they are and what they are about. The problem set between the words written and practical action of the men of the brotherhood. They stood each meeting and read who they are, and what they are about, but when you look at their action on how they were to operate; they did not practice what they were preached. If they could not live their belief in who they are, they would have to make some changes. The district association had no intentions to have anything to do with the brotherhood, but he wanted them to operate as a top brotherhood in the state and national. He wanted the men to stand tall, with knowledge, wisdom, understanding in the state and national, and live a love that only God could give. Having lived through a born again experience that rode well with true repentance.

A thought came across his mind due to a situation that happen in Dallas, Texas. A group of people peacefully left a church and started their own church. The then Cap/Rock district association refused to respond to their need of assistance. The request was made to the national and district and they was refused. The reason being, the new church did not have a pastor. The one thing that he wanted to make clear to the district association; He wanted them

to know that the district was there to support them. If a church was without a pastor, they would send an associate minister who had pastured a church before, but did not desire to pastor again. He must be a people person who really loved God's people. He had to be situational sound in word, prayer, and ministering.

It will be the same if a church split and is without a pastor, the district will oversee the church, and give them all the instructions that they need. The district will not help them find a pastor, but will guide them with the word toward calling a pastor. He must be strong on finance, a Sunday School scholar. His preaching style should be from teaching to a little hoop to tickle the imagination. The length of time to wait before looking for a pastor rest on the shoulders of the church membership.

Rev. King, The Moderator, the leader of the Cap/Rock District association, has more coming up on his plate than what he can handle. He is aware that the responsibility of this group of churches should never have been presented to any one man for leadership. He thought to himself, that Baptist Churches throughout history have sought blessings that flow from a voluntary fellowship with sister churches. He kind of smiled to himself; these groups of churches are called associations. The object is not a centralizing of power or of finance. No extensive organization is established. Fellowship and mutual help in missionary activity and other common tasks purely voluntary. The association must not violate the sovereign independence of the local church.

There are definite benefits to our association fellowships. There is a real danger to local churches in isolationism. A church by itself may either become proud with a feeling that it alone is true to the Lord, or it may swing to the opposite extreme in discouragement because the task is too great and there are none to help. It is both humbling and encouraging to fellowship with sister churches and find them faithful, fruitful works for the Lord. These fellowships, or associations, are a means of strength to accomplish some things which cannot be done separately. This is especially true in out missionary work. Smaller churches share in tasks which they could not undertake alone.

Rev. King changed position in his car, there were something coming to his mind that was not clear. The term association is used in TWO distinct and quite dissimilar senses; by not observing which fact much confusion, and at times no small difficulty, arises in the minds of people. O yes, he thought, the association is used in two distinct and quite dissimilar senses; First the organized body which meets annually for the transaction of business, is called an association. This body corporate consist of PASTORS and MESSENGERS; as its constituent element and active members. It has its constitution, by-laws, its order of business, meets and adjourns, publishes its proceeding, enrolling the names of the pastors and messengers, who alone have the rights of membership in its session.

Second, in a somewhat vague and ideal sense all the associated churches, and the geographical limits over which they are scattered, are called the ASSOCIATION. Thus we speak of the dearth or the prosperity which prevail in this are that association, or we say that revivals have, or have not been extensive in such or such an association. No reference is here had to the organic body which meets annually for business, but to the territorial field, and the local Church's from which the pastor and messengers come.

An association---the organized body that meets for business--is not composed of churches, but of individuals, the pastor and messengers. It is a common way of speaking, but a very loose and misleading way, to say it composed of churches. This arises from a misapprehension, and perpetuates a misunderstanding. A Baptist Church cannot be a member of any other body whatever. It would violate its sacred charter, and lose its identity as the body of Christ, to attempt such a union. If many churches should enter into organic relation, and constitute an ecclesiastical confederation, the local church would be absorbed, loosing largely their individuality and their independence.

But it may be asked, how is it, if churches are not MEMBERS

of the body, that the Association uniformly receive new churches to their numbers, or dismiss, or drop churches from it? The reply is this, churches are not received to MEMBERSHIP, though such expression are often, and indeed ordinarily used; but they are received to FELLOWSHIP AND cooperation; which in fact is evinced, by their pastors and messengers being admitted to MEMBERSHIP, thus composing its constituent elements.

An association is not a REPRESENATIVE body, in the ordinary acceptation of the term. A Baptist Church cannot appoint persons with delegate authority to act for it, so as to bind it by their action. It cannot transfer its authority and responsibility to any person, or persons whatever. It can appoint persons as committees to perform service for it and report their doings. If it be still insisted, for the sake of terms, that the churches do meet in the association, by their representatives, the pastors and messengers, the reply must be---such is not the case, and cannot be, either actually or constructively for a Baptist Church cannot be REPRESENTED by delegates authorized to act for it in any organization whatever.

An association is a voluntary society formed and maintained for mutual health among the churches associated, and for the religious welfare of the field it occupies. It is of human, not of divine authority; it grows out of the sympathies of Christian fellowship, and the need of mutual health. No church is under obligation to affiliate with it; and any connected church can withdraw cooperation, at any time,, and any reason which seem to itself sufficient, without prejudice to either its evangelical or its denomination reputation and standing. But while it continues associated, it must abide by the rules and regulations, mutually agreed upon, by which the body is governed.

Because an Association is not a representative body, and because a church cannot be represented in any other organization, and because a church cannot, even if it would, alienate, or transfer its powers and responsibilities to any man, or body of men, therefore an association cannot legislate for the churches, exercise any authority over them, or bind them in any way by its own action. Whatever is done while in session, is od authority only to those who do it. That is the members--pastor and delegate's. They may make suggestions to the churches, or present appeals, and lay request before them; to all of which the churches will give such attention as may seem to them right and proper.

The fact that the messengers are appointed by their respective churches argues nothing as to their being invested with the delegated power. This appointment is made at the request of the Association, and according to its constitutional provisions, as the most convenient and equitable methods of constituting the body, not because the appointment carries any ecclesiastical authority with it. These messengers bear the letters and salutations of their churches, and consult with the other members as to the objects for the interest of which they meet.

The association is an independent body, not subject to the authority or control of the churches any more than the churches are subject to its authority and control. It frames its own constitution, makes its own by-laws, elect it own officers, and manage its own business, without dictation from anyone. Within its own sphere of action it is just as independent as a church is within its sphere of action. It fixes the term of membership and the condition of which the churches may associate; designate the number of messengers to be sent to each church, order its own exercises, meets and adjourns at its own pleasure. If any church did not approve the proceeding it can refuse to affiliate, and withdraw at any time from the association, if it thinks best.

In the exercise of its independence, also, the Association can refuse to receive its messengers, and drop from its fellowship any church that has violated the constitution and the original compact, or that has, in any matter deemed vital, departed from the faith and practice of the associated churches and the denomination. Provision for such emergencies are made in the constitution of all Associations; also the process of fraternal labor to be pursued with the recusant Church before final excision shall be decreed is likewise prescribed.

\Rev. King mind was backed with information, instructions and maybe even commands directly from God. What he needed now is some time by himself, to think, pray, wonder, and let the Lord talk to him. He is thankful of the people that the Lord have sent his way. HE KNOW NOW THAT HE WILL NOT HAVE TO MAKE ALL THE IMPORTANT DECISIONS, God has given him help that he can trust, and there are other help who have no idea that they will be working with the Association.

Rev. King set his cruse control on 75 mph and headed his car toward home. Home where he and his family reside, and home for the Cap/Rock District Association. He did not close his eyes, he just battered them a couple of times. It was then that he saw the most beautiful valley that he had ever seen.

It was deep, but there were a winding road that lead to the other side of the valley. For a moment he could not see the highway, only the valley that lie ahead of him. It was deep and it had everything that God had created in its place. The rivers, the lakes, the ponds, green vegetation all over the valley. Thought there was a way to the other side, it was not clear. Everything about the valley was complicated, nothing was clear, nothing was simple, every thing stood as a challenge to his well being. Without a complete understanding it confused the mind, and brought in doubt, where doubt was not necessary. He then remembered that this is the Valley of Human Struggle and as long as he is moderator of the Cap/Rock District Association he will feel the pain of human struggle even though he cannot visualized the valley of the struggle in his mind.

But what he can remember seem to be out of place, it's kind of like Jabez prayer, it come out of no where with meaning that is hard to understand. But this was the third time since he was selected as moderator that this thought had been burned into his mind. It was the word of Jesus, "Therefore whoever eats this bread and drink this cup of the Lord in an unfitting way is guilty of a sin against his body and blood of the Lord. But let a man examine himself, and so let him eat of that bread and drink of that cup. For he who eats and drinks as some of you do, eats and drinks judgment to himself, because he does not discern what the body mean. It is because of this that many among you are ill and weak and some have died.

But if we truly discern what we are like we will not be liable to judgment. But in this very judgment of the Lord we are being disciplined that we may not be finally condemned alone with the world." Moderator King thought to himself that was God speaking to him, and it would be necessary for him to listen carefully. He thought for a moment that there is no passage in the whole New Testament is of greater interest than this. For one thing, it give us our warrant for the most sacred act of worship in the Church, the Sacrament of the Lord's supper; and for another the letter to the Corinthians is earlier than the earliest of the gospels, this is actually the first recorded account we possess of any word of Jesus. He set before us a covenant, and a covenant is a relationship entered into between two people.

The Cap/Rock District Association must teach the basics where that each person desires to live the life they learn in our class rooms. Most likely the Sacrament can never mean the same thing for every person; but we do not need fully to understand everything about the Sacrament to benefit from it. For all that we do well to try at least to understand something of what Jesus meant when he spoke of the bread and the wine as he did.

"This is my body," He said of the bread. One simple fact precludes us from taking this with a crude literalism. When Jesus spoke, he was still in the body; and there was nothing clearer than that his body and the bread were at that moment quite different things. Nor did he simply mean, "this stand for my body." In a sense that is true. The broken bread of the Sacrament does stand for the body of Christ; but it does more. To him who takes it into his hands and upon his lips with faith and love, it is a means not only of memory but of living contact with Jesus Christ. To an unbeliever it would be nothing; to a lover of Christ it is the way to his presence.

"This cup," said Jesus, in the usual version, "is the new covenant in my blood." Let us translate it slightly different. "This cup is the new covenant and it cost my blood." Now a covenant is a relationship entered into between two people. There was an old covenant between God and man and that old relationship was based on the law. In it God chose and approached the people of Israel and became a special sense their God; but there were a condition, that, if this relationship was going to last, they must keep his law. With Jesus a new relationship is open to man, dependent not on law but on love, dependent not on man's ability to keep the law—for no man can do that—but on the free grace of God's love of God's love offered to men.

This passage goes on to talk about eating and drinking this bread and wine unworthily. The unworthiness consisted in the fact that the man who did so did "not discern the Lord's body>" That phrase can equally well mean two things; and each is so real and so important that it is quite likely that both are intended.

(1) It may mean that the man who eats and drinks unworthily does not realize what the sacred symbols mean. It may mean that he eats and drinks with no reverence and no sense of the love that these symbols stand for or the obligation that is laid upon him.

(2) It may also mean this. The phrase THE BODY OF CHRIST again and again stand for the church. Paul in his letter to the church has just been rebuking those who with their division and their class distinction divide the Church; so this may mean that he eats and drinks unworthily who has never realized that the whole church is the body of Christ but is at variance with his brother. Every man in who's heart there is hatred, bitterness, contempt against his brother man, as he comes to the table of our Lord, eats and drinks unworthily. So then he eats and drinks unworthily is to do so with no sense of the greatness of the thing we do, and to do so while we are at variance with the brother for whom also

Christ died. If the table of Christ were only for sinless people none might even approach it. The way is never closed to the penitent sinner. To the man who loves God and his fellow men the way is ever open, and his sins, thought they be as scarlet, shall be white as snow.

No sooner that he blinked and the valley was there, he blanked and the valley had gone into the wind that had brought it forth. But the supper troubled him. This supper that we partake of one Sunday out of a month, lingered for a while, because the church had found herself in misunderstanding and disobedience. Many church members find themselves tied to thread of un-repented sin because of their disobedient. It is not always intentional, some time out of ignorance; people just don't know or understand the words of God for their life.

Rev. King thought for a moment. There was no doubt that he had been caught up in the valley of struggle. A valley that lay between un-repented sin and true repentance. He found himself emotional, he knew of some friends of his who had been caught in the valley. They are so sure that they are right until they will not listen to reason. But he had a message that must be delivered, even if it cost him his life. He thought to himself; the man who would bring an effective message to others must first receive it from God, the King's message was repent.

To repent means to change one's mind; and then to fit one's action to this change. Yes, it is a change of heart and a change of action it is bount for it involves the bitter realization that the way we were following is wrong. It is bound to disturb, because it means complete reversal of life. Repentance is no sentimental feeling sorry. Repentance is a revolutionary thing—that is why so few repent.

He remembered a scripture in the book of Mark 6:12-13, "So they went out and heralded forth the summons to repented and they cast out demons, and anointed many sick people with oil and healed then." He thought to himself, here lie's the challenge of our association, if we don't meet the challenge the association will not be successful. The teaching in today's churches does not prepare us for the task that lie ahead of us.

He was a little shaken of the troubling supper and yet the beautiful sight that he had seen. He was a little nervous and unsteady until God spoke to him through 2 Peter1:3-7. "Since His divine power has bestowed upon us all things that are necessary for true life and true religion, through the knowledge of him who called us to His own glory and excellence, and since through these gifts there heave been bestowed upon us precious and very great promises, that through them we might escape the world's corruption cause by lust, and become sharers in the divine nature since all this is so, bend all your energy to the task of equipping your faith with courage, your courage with knowledge, your knowledge with self-control, your self-control with steadfastness, your steadfastness with piety, your piety with brotherly affection, your brotherly affection with Christian Love." He thought for a moment; If tomorrows struggle, suffering and tribulation will hold onto its own tomorrow; let the wind and the rabbit search for this presence present tomorrow, in today's world of survival, give us wisdom to love and be obedient to our father's this today. He looked at the sign that read 35 North, he kind of chuckled to himself. I am still in my lane.

on the side of the road was his animal friends, they were running alone with the car, then together they turned and went west. On their way to help someone else. They never looked back, they never stopped or slowed, they never looked down, never said a word.

They were on their way to help a God sent man who had been caught in the valley of human struggle. They just kept rocking into the western sun-set to help someone else. They may have been a little over due, but they would get there in time.